Life Skills for Your ADHD Teen

Coping Skills and Life Lessons to Prepare Your Teen
for The Emotional World Ahead

Kenneth Harvey

Disclaimer Notice:

Please note the information contained within this document is for educational and entertainment purposes only. All effort has been executed to present accurate, up-to-date, reliable, and complete information. No warranties of any kind are declared or implied. Readers acknowledge that the author is not engaged in the rendering of legal, financial, medical, or professional advice. The content within this book has been derived from various sources. Please consult a licensed professional before attempting any techniques outlined in this book.

By reading this document, the reader agrees that under no circumstances is the author responsible for any losses, direct or indirect, that are incurred as a result of the use of the information contained within this document, including, but not limited to, errors, omissions, or inaccuracies.

I Dedicate These Books To My Daughter Who Has Opened My Mind To Learning More About ADHD And Encouraging Me To Write This Book To Help Other Parents Struggling To Understand ADHD

Contents

Have Something Near You At All Times That Can Give You the Time

Create A Timesheet

Have Them Do Work In Their Peak Productivity Time

Leave Free Time In Their Day To Day Schedule

Prioritize Your Day

Get Enough Sleep

Make Sure That the Schedule Is Enjoyable

Try Not To Make Too Many Changes

Choose the Time Frame You Are Scheduling

Have A Schedule For the Weekends Too

To-Do List

Pay Attention To How, When, and How Long They Procrastinate

Add Something To Mundane Tasks To Make It Interesting

Try Not To Look Over Their Shoulder

Goal Setting

Organization Tips For ADHD

Limit How Long You Spend On Decisions

Try Not To Do Too Much

Work Together

Keep Everything Bright And Visual

Help Your Teen Fight Clutter

Manage The Number Of Projects Your Teen Is Trying To Do

Use A Timer To Organize

This has the power to benefit everyone in your home, and it's a great thing for your teen later. Find Some Different Organization Methods Online With Your Teen

Is Your Teen Kind To Themself?
Have Patience

Introduction

I want you to imagine, for a moment, an average day in Jennifer's life. Jennifer is the mother of sixteen-year-old Trinity. In Jennifer's eyes, Trinity is perfect, and she is truly sweet and caring. She's managed to make money by making and selling jewelry and has an absolutely magnetic personality.

Trinity also has ADHD, and that has contributed to several issues that worry Jennifer. As she goes downstairs, she can't help but notice that Trinity is in the same clothes as yesterday and hasn't brushed her hair. Jennifer doesn't have to ask to know that she didn't take a shower or brush her teeth. Trinity is on her phone, waiting to flip a pancake. Jennifer jumps in to flip it after starting to smell it burn. Even though the pancake is black, Trinity rolls her eyes. She counters with a "mom, it's fine. I can cook for myself!"

After putting the issue to rest and enjoying breakfast, Trinity rushes around, grabbing homework, keys, and other things she knows she will need. Jennifer sighs and rubs her eyes, and this was something she was supposed to have done last night.

"Where's your lunch?" she has to ask. Trinity stops, shrugs and says she will pick something up to go from the nearest chain coffee shop. She shrugs off her mother's concerns about her having enough money for that.

Finally, they both head out the door. Jennifer notices that Trinity is entering the school into google maps before she takes off. While Jennifer knows that she will at least make it to school, she worries. Trinity has been going to the same school this whole time, and she's been driving for over a month. How does she not know the way?

During the day, Jennifer gets a notification that Trinity was late to her homeroom. The teacher took particular offense. After all, she was clearly late because she went to get coffee. She also got a text from her daughter, asking to grab a piece of homework that she'd forgotten.

Jennifer loved her daughter and knew that she'd make the world a better place, but she was really worried. Her daughter was sixteen, and there were still some critical life skills that she seemed to lack. How did she make sure that her daughter got those skills before she left? Trinity was already talking about college, so it was only a matter of time.

To Jennifer, it felt like there were so many things to go over in such a short amount of time, and she didn't know where to start. On the one hand, she knew that her daughter had the hardcore skills to make it in life. Her personality would take her far. She had passion, and heck, she even had her own little business together. But what about some of the softer things and the essential skills that one needs. Trinity can't afford to always grab something from the nearest coffee shop for a meal. She won't be there when the food is burning. She won't be there if Trinity needs someone to run her the homework. And that just touched on a couple of the issues she noticed today. What should she do?

The number of things we need to teach our little ones as they grow into adults can feel overwhelming. As we go through life, the world isn't going to care about whether you have attention-deficit/hyperactivity disorder (ADHD) or you don't. As cold as it is to say, it is the reality that we find ourselves in, and our kids will find themselves there too. It's our job as parents to worry about how they will do and teach them what they need to know.

In the future, our kids will know how to present themselves. They will learn how to keep themselves healthy. They will understand how to plan and manage things, and they will be able to remember everything as they walk out the door. The key is for us to give that guidance while they still live under our roof and not wait for the world to provide them with that guidance first.

There are many books out there that talk about how to give these skills to your teen. It talks about how to teach them to do things they will need to know, and it often outlines strategies you can use. The trouble with these books is that they are based on teens who don't have ADHD. Therefore, many of the teaching strategies may not work.

This book is designed to help with precisely that. I want to give you strategies that will work with your soon-to-be adult, and I also want to take the chance to highlight some unique adulting struggles that someone with ADHD might face. I know that it can feel frustrating when you have this monumental task ahead of you, and while some people have many resources to combat this problem, it seems you have relatively few.

I started this journey when there was even less information about ADHD than there is now. My daughter was diagnosed at a young age, and like you, I wanted to be there for her and support her. Most importantly, I didn't want her to leave my house without knowing how to be a functional adult with the ability to aim for her dreams.

With no resources readily available, I dove in deep. I did research, and I attended other classes. I got to know parents who also have children with ADHD and were also trying to raise children that could thrive in the world ahead of them. This has all amounted to over ten years of experience study-ing and learning from other parents, and I want to share my knowledge. I'm excited to pass on my knowledge in a way so that everyone can access it. Information about ADHD and how to handle it while still raising successful human beings shouldn't be so hard to come by.

We're going to start this book with the basics. Self-care is vital but easy to neglect, especially when you have ADHD.

Chapter One

Self Care and Grooming

If your kiddo has ADHD, then this is probably a battle you've been at for a long time. Taking care of one's personal hygiene doesn't come naturally to many people and can be time-consuming and annoying. For someone with ADHD, it still takes long enough to do these tasks.

When you and your kiddo talk about personal hygiene, you've probably heard them mention that it just takes too much time and they'd rather be doing other things. You've also probably heard that no one is going to notice or really care, so why should they bother? This might be especially true if they plan to be home that day.

The other things you hear might relate to sensory issues or issues with cleanliness, which is common for someone with ADHD.

Jennifer knows that some of Trinity's complaints are that the toothpaste is too spicy, showers are too hot, and conversely, getting out of the water is too cold.

Finally, there is the tell-tale "I forgot," which may or may not be true.

Whatever the case, hygiene is important in making sure that they are presentable to the world, and more importantly, it keeps us from getting sick.

So, how do we make sure that our kids can really implement good hygiene practices before they leave the nest?

General Hygiene Tips and Tricks

Area 1: Brushing Your Teeth

Tip: Technology

It's the 21st century, so the fact that technology comes into play when we brush our teeth shouldn't be a surprise to me... but it is.

For parents with kids that really struggle, there are toothbrushes that connect to apps, which will help remind your teen that their teeth need to be brushed, time them and track how they are doing in getting every side brushed. This tech can absolutely help keep them on top of things!

It's also expensive! Some similar things you can do is have them make use of their phone to track how long they are brushing their teeth, and they can further divide the time if they aren't getting their sides evenly. Using a habit tracker can also encourage them to get their teeth brushed. There are simple ones and more complex ones that have you take care of something like a plant or penguin based on your completion of daily tasks.

Area 2: Caring For Your Body

Tip: Make it Visual

This works for just about anything. Having visual charts, rather than having something written out, can make a big difference in how things are processed. Simply put, you don't have to read a line of text to remember what's going on.

You can have a visual chart for showers, teeth brushing, face and hair care, and more. Furthermore, these schedules can be made by you and your teen, which can add to the willingness to follow if they are artistically inclined. You can also print out a simple one on Pinterest, or many sights make buyable versions. Whatever best helps you and your teen is your best bet!

Tip: Ask Them To Tell You What to Do... Backward

Have you ever had a tough test that you needed to memorize something for, so, in order to nail it, you memorize the process backward (fun fact: my teacher had us do this for the photosynthesis cycle)? You can do this with hygiene practices to help them remember. If they are struggling, go over the process with them a few times. Have them write it down in the correct order, then ask them to recite what they've just been taught backward. It's okay if it takes several tries, but typically, if you can do something backward, then it will work in the opposite direction too!

Tip: Repetition

One thing we will talk about a lot in this book is the process of natural consequences. Children with ADHD rarely learn the "why" of important behaviors when punishment is used. In fact, punishment may get you what has been termed as "instant obedience," but it will rarely get you what you really want, which is long-term learning. Punishment may even lead to an explosion later on, as children with ADHD don't have the best regulation abilities. This is something we want to avoid.

On the other hand, natural consequences illustrate a cause-and-effect relationship that the child can hold on to. In this case, the cause might be that they didn't properly shower or brush their teeth, and they need to be clean, so the effect is that they have to do it again.

If one of your teens' complaints is that it takes too long, then this lesson is going to stick fast.

Now, this might not work as well on older teens, and if it's still a struggle, it might be good to switch to a new tactic.

The effects of long-term lack of care are warned about in doctor and dentist offices, and the information is readily available online. Please share it with your teen, and let them know that there are reasons that personal care is essential and that, while it's annoying, it needs to be practiced.

Tip: Acknowledge Where the Difficulties Lay

No one likes being told that they aren't keeping up with their hygiene, especially when they are teenagers. It can result in some self-esteem issues, which is something that those with ADHD are more prone to. Remind them that, yes, it is just their ADHD getting in the way. It's okay for them to need more time to focus on it, and it's expected. There are still some things that they can do better than others because of their ADHD, and this might just be a struggling area.

Take Trinity, for example. She is, admittedly, one of the few students in her class that struggle with hygiene. But, every single one of her teachers has mentioned that she is animated. She's interesting to talk to and listen to, and she is one of the best presenters in her class. To top it all off, Trinity is building her own small business at age 18. How many teens do you know fit that?

Your teen might be annoyed that they have to pull away from something they were working on that they found really interesting. Acknowledge that as a valid feeling. It may not change the outcome of the situation, but it sucks!

Validate their issues with their senses. We may still have to shower, but maybe it really is too hot or too cold. If that's what they say, then try to work on strategies that help them reduce this issue.

In Trinity's case, she found the toothpaste her mom bought to be "too spicy." The minty flavor was too strong, and it hurt her mouth. Trinity's mom decided to switch brands for her, and she instantly noticed that the complaints all but stopped.

Finally, there's an important distinction to be made between actually being lazy or just having ADHD. When you have ADHD, you might not want to shower because of the reasons we just talked about, it could be because you are busy, or it could be something else entirely. It's rarely because a person is lazy. Making that distinction can be very preventative when it comes to fighting against low self-esteem.

What Problems Might Be Causing the Issue?

You will probably get an answer whenever you ask why they might not make hygiene practices a regular habit. The question is, is it the answer you need or the one they want you to hear?

There are many reasons why they might choose not to have a shower or brush their teeth. Let's take a look at some of the more common causes that we find when we dig deeper.

The Lack of Dopamine

The brain of someone with ADHD doesn't have as much dopamine as an average person. Dopamine is what is needed for the brain to function, and it's essentially the chemical that controls our motivation. When it comes to performing hygiene functions, dopamine will be pretty low. This alone is likely a huge part of your battle.

There are some ways you can replace that dopamine. Rewards are the most obvious way to do it. Creating a system where their efforts are rewarded can increase dopamine levels significantly. Rewards can be as simple as a piece of candy, a dollar, or a promise to play their favorite game. Each child will be different. See about sitting down and talking to yours about what might work for them.

Relating to dopamine deficiency is depression. Dopamine is also one of the chemicals responsible for happiness; a severe lack of it can lead to depression. When dealing with depression, not only is the brain struggling to create dopamine at a certain level, but it's also struggling to replenish it, and even risk-taking behaviors may not give a hit.

At this point, rewards might not help. Keep an eye out for depressive symptoms. When they last longer than two weeks and impact a person's daily functioning and overall quality of life, then they are said to have clinical depression.

In these cases, seeking help from a professional can make all of the difference! They can help you come up with strategies for routines and depression management. If needed, they can also recommend medication that can help!

Having a Set Schedule

Ask yourself, what does having a set schedule do for you?

For many of us, it creates balance. It helps us know what is going on next in our day, and it helps us make sure we get everything done.

Imagine, for a moment, not having any kind of schedule and finding sticking to them nearly impossible. This is often a huge struggle for those with ADHD. Their brain doesn't naturally stick to a schedule, making it very hard to stick with a plan in their day, and this includes making time for general hygiene practices.

When dealing with this, someone with ADHD isn't likely to make brushing their teeth or getting a shower their top priority.

When helping someone with ADHD create a schedule, it should first be in a place they check daily. A planner will work if they are likely to look at it. Other places include their bedroom wall, the fridge in the kitchen, or the lock screen of their phone, tablet, or computer. Making these schedules visual, instead of writing them out, will also make them easier to follow. The schedule should also include things they want to do to motivate them to stick to it. Finally, the schedules should be as simple as possible so that they are easy to read.

Lack Of Attention To the Clock

We might all have days when we don't pay attention to the clock and lose track of time. Someone with ADHD is much more prone to this than we might be. They may be in a phase of distraction, or they may be hyper-focused. Either way, it might be hours before they check the clock again.

In the case of your teen, they might get started on either their homework or another project. They get a good groove going, and all of a sudden, it's 10 p.m. They know they should shower and brush their teeth, but they are tired, so they go straight to bed.

It can be difficult to interrupt your child when they have a good flow going, especially when it's what they are supposed to do. That being said, it is important to ensure your child is doing regular hygiene practices to build a strong habit.

In this case, having timers set on their phone will make them look at the clock and remind them that it's time to step away from work and toward the shower.

If your teen has a tendency just to turn off the reminder and continue working, then you can set the timer on your phone or be mindful of the time and remind them about 15 minutes after the timer has passed.

Overstimulation

The final issue I want to discuss is overstimulation. Overstimulation is another common issue for someone with ADHD.

When you have ADHD, your brain tends not to regulate emotions as well as sensory input. When it receives too much, it might not tune it out the way an average person would, and it might also be hyper-fixate on the small things.

We discussed that Trinity felt like the toothpaste burned her mouth in one example. Other people might find a shower overstimulating or something like wet hair hanging on their back triggering. Simply put, there are many things that can create this issue.

The best solution is often to sit down with your kiddo and discuss these. Ask them what the hygiene process feels like, if it's too much, and try to dig deeper into why. Not everyone will have the language about overstimulation at hand in their minds and ready to go, so you may have to do some digging or present the topic of overstimulation and what it means before you settle down to discuss it.

Once you and your kiddo narrow down what might be causing the problem, try to look for a solution. If the toothpaste is too minty, get a different one. You can even try kids' toothpaste if it will help, as it's made to do the same thing and often has a fruity flavor. If the feeling of a shower is too much, try a bath. Solutions that minimize or take care of the issue can be discussed if it's something after the fact, like wet hair.

Additional Steps and Tips

Patience Is Key

In this situation, patience is going to be your best friend. It will probably take time to make regular hygiene practices a consistent habit. There will be some great days, some relapses, and days where they just refuse. Don't give in but make it a habit to remain gently firm.

Discuss the Issue

It might be a surface-level thing, like overstimulation or simply trouble sticking to a schedule. These issues have solutions that can make the battle a much easier one for you.

As children become teens, this discussion step is also great for helping them with their desires for independence and being treated like adults.

Accept That Some Things Might Be Out Of Your Control

Your child is a teen now, and they have more agency and autonomy over their body. At this point, you cannot exactly forcibly put them in the shower, and you cannot forcibly brush their teeth. If it is at a point where they are genuinely upset and having a meltdown about the situation, then let it go. It's harming them and you mentally. You can always start the next day.

What you can control is holding them accountable. Verbal reminders, withholding rewards, and if they are younger, making them go back and try again if their work wasn't adequate are all things that can help manage the situation.

Ask the Deeper Questions

First, is there a physical reason they don't want to shower or brush their teeth?

Some children have very sensitive gums, so when they are brushed, they bleed. This might freak them out, and it might be painful.

Is the soap they are using okay? Do they show any signs of being allergic? Does it make their skin itch? Find out.

Next, let's talk about the mental health side of hygiene. First of all, if someone is doing poorly with their mental health, then proper hygiene is often the first thing to go.

We talked a little about depression already. Anxiety can be another factor. If your teen has anxiety tied to certain aspects of hygiene maintenance, then pushing the issue might be hurting them. Talk to them about this, especially if you notice signs of anxiety or panic setting in. A professional can advise on strategies that will help.

Having "Talks"

If your child isn't a fan of hygiene practices and doesn't understand why they are important, they will fight tooth and nail against it.

In order to get them in on your efforts, you may need to sit them down and explain why you are taking these steps.

Explain that basic hygiene needs to be done regularly, or else things tend to build up. Let them know hygiene can prevent sickness and infections, and it helps with body odor and acne.

Try to set up a separate time and space to have this conversation. Having it in the middle of an argument will likely result in your words not being taken seriously.

Sit down at a time that differs from when they are supposed to shower or get ready for bed. Lay out your talking points and be prepared to discuss them in detail.

As your child grows and develops, understanding this will be important. If this is an area your teen struggles with, as many teens do, these steps can help!

Chapter Two

Keeping Them Healthy

Collin's birthday is only a few months away. At 18, he will be leaving in about six months for college. While Collin does well in many ways, his parents have one major concern.

Collin has never cared much about what goes into his body. He rarely feels like cooking, so he will often grab a snack that is less than healthy and sit down to eat it. His mother has tried to talk to him about the dangers of this and how cooked food is often better for him, but Collin brushes off her concerns.

His family is also concerned with the exercise level Collin displays. He will often play video games for a long time, which his parents have accepted as his primary interest, but he rarely goes outside to exercise.

His parents are really looking to set him on the right track, but they are running out of time.

Diet and exercise are important to everyone's health, especially for those with ADHD.

The frontal lobe of the brain of someone who has ADHD is often functioning at a reduced capacity. Diet and exercise, however, can significantly improve a person's brain function. Making sure that one is eating healthy and getting some activity can go a long way in ensuring that they remain healthy and can also improve their functioning.

So, how do we instill these habits before they leave?

The short answer is action-based encouragement. By actively modeling behaviors and encouraging them to get involved, you set them up for success later in life!

Diet

Healthy eating is something that much of the world struggles with, and many of us are just... busy. Like Collin, we gravitate toward ready-made foods because it's easier, and they are already there. We need to work on changing this as much as possible.

Why Is It So Important to Have a Healthy Diet Plan?

First, let's start with the benefits.

By eating a highly varied, natural diet, you are aiding your mind and body.

Physically, by eating a healthy diet, your body will run better, and you will have an easier time getting up, moving around, and enjoying being alive. It's important to note that weight has little bearing on this. People on two opposite ends of the BMI spectrum may function relatively similarly if they both eat healthy diets.

Physically, it will help you live longer as well. A healthy diet has been continuously linked to a longer life span and more enjoyment of that life.

Now mentally, a healthy diet can add clarity to your thoughts. It sharpens your focusing power and can improve your attention span, especially when ADHD is involved. Furthermore, it can have a positive impact on your overall mental health. With the increased brain function, your brain can create chemicals like dopamine more easily.

Now, what can happen if we follow a poor diet in our lifetime?

You might first run into heart disease and its associated conditions. A diet high in things like red meat, saturated fats, and sweets can lead to a heart attack happening much earlier in life.

This is because a lot of the fat and sugar get stuck while they are carried along by the bloodstream. These fat deposits start small, but they can build up over time, leading to high cholesterol levels. Because these deposits are building up, your blood has to work harder to make it through your arteries, leading to high blood pressure. The next thing you have to worry about is a heart attack, as the fat deposits can build to where they close up an artery completely. A heart attack will happen when the blood cannot reach the heart.

The link is less studied, but poor diet has also been associated with various cancers, including lung and liver cancer. Fat deposits in both organs (which is a scary thought in itself) are believed to play a huge role.

Does this mean that you are automatically destined to suffer this fate if you eat steak? Not at all. A diet takes a long time to have this big of an effect on the body. Many people reach their 40s before they start to notice that there's anything wrong, and it doesn't take a toll until they are about 50 or 60. Genetics is also a factor.

You can still eat these foods in moderation as well. You may still have that piece of chocolate cake, just not every single day.

The younger your teen is introduced to this information, the better, but no age is too late.

Use pictures and visuals, like food pyramids and bodily circulatory systems, to break the information down. By making it visual, you are more likely to make this information stick.

Once you discuss the *why* with your teen, it's time to move on to the *how*. After all, this information is great, but it doesn't address a plan on what to do.

Use a Plan Like MyPlate

It's interesting that with the creation of so many fad diets (Paleo, Keto, Whole 30, and intermittent fasting, just to name a few), the healthiest thing for our bodies is still outlined in the government resource known as MyPlate. Unlike fad diets, which can be created by anyone with an internet connection and a small amount of knowledge of the body, MyPlate was created with input from dieticians all across the country. Most countries will have a very similar resource specific to their nation (and their nation's food supply) that people can access, and MyPlate is the American version of this eating plan.

MyPlate and its international cousins are visual. For those with ADHD, a visual of what's going on can help them follow it. For additional guidance, you can write out exactly how much is needed and recommended in each little section on the chart.

So, how much of each group is recommended? For teens who are 14 years of age or more and have a need for about 2000 calories a day, these are the numbers. If your child is a bit younger or their calorie needs are different, then these numbers might vary slightly, and the information can be found on myplate.gov.

For fruits, about two cups a day is recommended. It's stressed that it doesn't really matter what form the fruits are found in; it just matters that it is pure fruit. Fresh fruit is fine, and so is canned or frozen fruit. Fruit juice is good too, so long as it's 100% fruit juice and no additional sugars are added. Fruits add vitamins and minerals to the diet that wouldn't be there otherwise. Some examples include fiber and vitamin C.

Next up are vegetables. It's recommended to have about 2 ½ cups of vegetables daily, slightly more than a person's fruit intake. These vegetables also add key vitamins and minerals to the diet and help with skin, eyesight, and heart health. Like fruits, you can have them in any form, but what is going to be important is having variety. Different vegetables will help your body do different things.

For example, if your two and a half cups of vegetables only consist of carrots, you are doing a huge favor for your eyesight and immune system. However, you are missing out on other nutrients, such as iron from spinach.

Next up is protein. The recommendation for this is five and a half ounces. This can come from a certain amount of meat; a single egg is considered an ounce. So is about a quarter cup of legumes (non-processed beans). Tofu is also in the protein group. One thing that MyPlate stresses are that these come from lean proteins (meaning that the protein contains less fat). These include chicken and other white meats like turkey, fish, eggs, tofu, and legumes. It primarily excludes red meat such as steak, lamb, and pork. Again, these are okay occasionally, but they shouldn't be a part of the everyday diet.

Next is dairy, where about 3 cups a day are recommended. Dairy includes cow's milk and things like cheese and yogurt. If your kiddo isn't a big milk drinker, do not fear, as there are other ways to get what you're looking for. Just make sure that they enjoy fruits and vegetables high in vitamin D and that they eat food like yogurt or cheese. If your child is lactose intolerant, then fortified soy milk has been enriched to contain the same benefits (just make sure they are fortified).

Finally, the last food group is grains. Many diets, including MyPlate, specify that the grain should be whole wheat or at least enriched. The reason for this is because grains from white items (white bread, white rice, noodles) have all been stripped of the vitamins and minerals they should contain. White products are generally easier to work with. Enriched items have had the necessities added back in, but they are still highly processed. Look out for products like whole wheat bread, noodles, and brown rice. MyPlate recommends that about six ounces of grains be consumed per day. For reference, about one slice of bread is one ounce.

MyPlate, as I stated above, is the diet that meets the needs of nearly everyone unless there are specific issues that need to be addressed. Many other diets may do long-term harm. For example, keto has been linked to heart disease because of the extremely high protein intake.

If your teen would like to explore options that aren't related to MyPlate, here are a few cultural diets that they can try. These diets have gained in popularity because the people in the regions that enjoy them have significantly lower rates of diet-related disease.

The Mediterranean Diet

The Mediterranean diet is native to the countries in Europe that surround the Mediterranean Sea, and this includes Spain, Greece, and Italy.

Interest in this diet plan began when people realized that, unlike the rest of the world, people in this area weren't suffering from heart disease, food-related cancers, or other sicknesses that have now been related to the consumption of certain types of food. Research in this area told people that their diet was the reason. They eat the exact same food we do, but there are certain things they do differently.

Organic foods in many countries tend to be very expensive, and they are sold in smaller quantities than food that has been chemically treated or genetically modified. This isn't the case in the Mediterranean region. Thanks to the sea and the climate, it's easier to grow fresh fruits and vegetables in this area, so many of their products are organic.

The way their diet is structured differs a lot as well. The main part of the diet is fruits and vegetables, and these are consumed with every meal and often (but not always) make up the main portion of the meal.

Next up are nuts and seeds, which the region has heavy access to and can add to almost anything.

Legumes and potatoes follow as next on the list. Legumes, which refer to non-processed beans like black beans, red kidney beans, lima beans, and many others, are a great source of protein, and these are a great way to have protein for those looking to eat less meat.

Fresh potatoes can be prepared in a variety of different ways, and they are a good source of carbs and very filling.

Speaking of carbs, the next thing that makes up a massive part of their diet is whole grains. The white grains that we discussed in the section above don't really have a place in the Mediterranean diet. Instead, things like bread, pasta, rice, and other foods created by grains are made with whole grains.

Next on the list are herbs and spices. We all like adding flavor to our food, and the Mediterranean diet makes plenty of room for this. Fresh herbs are a part of many recipes, and for those who still want more, you can just add a little spice.

You may have noticed that we've talked about meat very little so far. Unlike diets found in regions like America, meat isn't a massive part of every meal. The exception might be fish and shellfish. Thanks to the Mediterranean Sea, this region has a vast amount of seafood available. It's usually fresh as well since people may fish for it themselves, or it's bought quickly after the catch. Fish consumption may not be in every meal, but it is often a part of one's daily diet.

Olive oil is the final major component of the Mediterranean diet. Most cooking is done with lightly processed olive oil. It tends to be the healthiest oil to use, and it gives food a great flavor.

White meats, dairy, and eggs aren't consumed as often, but they are a part of the Mediterranean diet. Researchers say they are consumed anywhere from two times a week to once a day.

Finally, red meats and sweets don't play much of a role in the Mediterranean diet. They are consumed maybe once or twice a week. With fish being so plentiful and fresh fruit within reach, there is often no need to consume a lot of these.

Not only is the Mediterranean diet good for avoiding disease, but it can also improve brain health.

This diet isn't just about the foods you eat. It comes down to what you eat and how you eat it as well. Recipes for Mediterranean meals are a little different, but the food for it tastes fantastic.

If your child has trouble with MyPlate or wants to try something different, then this is a great alternative.

Asian Diet

Traditional Asian diets have also been explored as the rate of disease related to food consumption is very low. The foods traditionally found in Asian cultures are slightly more processed but not nearly as much as those that are found in other regions.

One thing that stands out and sets it apart from the Mediterranean diet is the large use of white rice. Not only does rice exist for use as, well, rice, but it's also used to create several products. There are rice noodles and rice paper, just to name a few. One way or another, you are bound to find rice in your diet by following their eating plan!

Grains of all types end up being a massive part of the diet as well. There's wheat, barley, corn, and more. Grains and rice make up the base of most Asian meals.

Next up are fruits, vegetables, nuts, seeds, and legumes. These also make up a massive part of the diet, and they are consumed with at least two out of three meals each day. Vegetable-based oils are their primary cooking oil as well.

Seafood is consumed with at least one meal a day. Since many Asian countries find that they either border the ocean or at the very least they have several rivers and water sources, they have plenty of fish. Like the Mediterranean region, it's easy to get a hold of when it's fresh, so it's a bigger part of their diet.

Dairy plays a bigger role in the Asian diet. With many milk products available, it's consumed on an almost daily basis.

White meats, eggs, and sweets are consumed once or twice a week. Red meat is consumed monthly at most.

Like the Mediterranean diet, the Asian diet has unique ways of cooking that differ from other regions of the world. It's absolutely worth checking out, even if you are just looking to try new things with your child.

A great perk about trying a healthy, culturally based diet is that you can engage your child's creativity. Letting them try things, learn different ways to cook, and discover new balances in how they eat can all add interest to eating healthy.

A massive part of cultural diets is also the exercise that goes into them. The Mediterranean lifestyle involves a lot of walking and biking. Asian lifestyles put a lot of emphasis on a zen-based exercise like yoga. Children often learn it from a young age.

Since exercise is also a huge part of health, we are going to talk about it next.

Exercise

Remember our previous story? Collin's parents are struggling to get him outside to exercise, and it worries them. They decide they are going to sit down with Collin and talk about the why.

Why Should We Engage In Exercise?

One of the most basic reasons exercise holds value is that it can be a social experience. If you attend a class, or just plan to do it with friends, or you engage in sports, you can find that a lot of people are there for the same reason you are, and you can connect with them.

Another reason to engage in regular exercise is that it can help you sleep better. Sleep has always been an essential part of regenerating our bodies. That being said, it seems that today, we always have so much to worry about that sleeping falls to the wayside. We are often too busy, or our minds can't stop spinning long enough for us to get some real rest. Exercise can help us out with the second one. It tires out the body, and the time spent is very therapeutic for your brain as well.

If you have been feeling drained lately, then exercise can help you with that too! Exercise gets your heart rate up, and by giving your mind a chance to get away from work, your head might be clearer. Something as simple as a morning walk can add a lot of energy to your day!

When it comes to conditions associated with ADHD, we often have to talk about depression and low self-esteem. Both are common issues that sufferers face. Regular exercise, even if it involves simply going for a walk, can help. Exercise sends off chemicals like serotonin and dopamine, which are motivation and mood-boosting chemicals. Exercising outside, in the sunlight, also impacts how we see things. It allows us a break, giving our minds a chance to relax. Finally, exercising is an act of taking care of our body. This alone makes us feel better and more confident in our bodies, even if nothing changes.

If you ever feel like doctors are pushing you to exercise, there is a good reason for it! Exercise is a preventative factor in staving off disease. Your body, and as a result, your immune system, will tend to be stronger. Exercise also encourages stronger blood flow and improves muscle tension. With exercise, decreased rates of heart disease, high blood sugar, high cholesterol levels, and other heart health-related conditions are all seen the more a person exercises. Another thing that sees a decrease is the risk of diabetes. Strokes are less common in those who regularly exercise as well. Additionally, exercise involves continuous movement, which can prevent problems like arthritis later in life. Because your body is naturally stronger in life, it can prevent falls from being detrimental.

Finally, the most obvious reason that many of us exercise is for weight control. Weight isn't everything when it comes to our health, but it is one factor that can be used to measure it. Exercise can help us at least keep a consistent weight and maybe even help us shed a few pounds.

With these reasons in hand, it's time to talk to your kiddo. When we talk about building up a habit of exercise for later in life, give them reasons why. If there is something on the list that they are struggling with or that they are particularly worried about in the future, then connect exercise to that. The exception to this is weight. Exercise can help, but if that is your teen's concern and they don't see the scale move, they might get discouraged.

How To Encourage Exercise

In addition to talking about the "why," illustrating the "how" can also be important. Here are a few ways.

Memberships to Gyms or Groups.

A gym membership, where they can go and work out, can help them at least have a place to go where there is equipment. They can use this to their heart's content. This can be especially helpful if your teen has a car. On rougher days when they need to get some energy out, they have a healthy place to do so. Some gyms offer classes in things like dance, weightlifting, and yoga. If your teen wants to try some of these out, then they can!

Make It Family Time

If exercise becomes a family activity, then that becomes additional encouragement. Your teen will feel less alone in their efforts, and as a family, you have more time to connect. Walks around the neighborhood or a game of ball or frisbee are some great examples of simple things you can do.

Video Game Exercise

Let's go back to Collin for a moment. He loves video games. He has a couple of different gaming systems. In their research, his parents came across some ideas that could help Collin.

Today there are a few gaming systems that come with an active component. The two most common are the Xbox and the Wii. Both systems have games that are designed around the idea of exercise. Many of us enjoy our screen time, and it is very possible to enjoy it actively.

Sports

One final great way to get your child into the habit of regularly exercising is to get them into a sport that they like. There is basketball, baseball, dance, soccer, swimming, and so many more out there. Sports absolutely allow for exercise. They also include a major social component. When you do these things with friends, you are much more likely to enjoy them.

These strategies illustrate some of the ways you can get your teen into a pattern of activity. Which one works best will depend on the person. When you sit down with your teen to talk about why it's important, it's also going to help if you address how this is going to be done.

What do they want to do? Is there a sport they want to try? Do they want to go to the gym? Do they want to spend more time as a family? If there is something they are leaning towards, try it. If it's something they already have an interest in, they are more likely to be invested in it.

Cooking

It's time to circle back to food, as it's a vital component of being healthy. Eating healthy and exercising are just two components of being a healthy person. Cooking is important, as it ties everything together very well.

Cooking is going to be a huge part of eating right. In order to have good, healthy food, you must know how to make it.

The activity of cooking food for oneself can have similar benefits to exercise. Teaching children and teens how to cook can be fun... or it could be a disaster. Next, we're going to discuss some ways to get your teen engaged in the process.

Tips For Creating Enthusiasm For Cooking

Get Their Thoughts and Opinions About What You Are Cooking

Introduce them to the process and ingredients behind meals that they and other members of the family enjoy. You can also look at trying new things and getting their help with it.

If you are looking to try something new, find a few recipes that sound really good, and ask your teen to look over them and choose one. You can get their help with picking ingredients up at the store too.

Being involved in the cooking process can stir curiosity, and it also makes a person more comfortable with the process.

Engage Your Minds Senses

We have five senses through which we explore the world. Cooking is very capable of engaging them all. When getting your ADHD teen interested in cooking or food, try engaging as many senses as you possibly can.

What do they see? This one seems pretty straightforward at first, but to get them more involved with this sense, add some color to the dish. Colored vegetables are the most popular way to do this.

Next, what can they touch? What textures are on the plate? What's the feeling of a well-cooked steak? What is the sauce like? There might be some sanitary concerns with this step, so you can limit it to their plate or have them describe what the textures would feel like to them.

The sound of cooking may not seem like it has much involvement in cooking until you are frying some vegetables or cooking meat on the grill. You can hear the sounds of sizzling as you cook food. You can hear the knife slide through different vegetables. All of these things can appeal to our sense of hearing.

The sense of smell is an important one in a kitchen, and asking your teen to stop and step into the kitchen with their eyes closed, ready to pick up that scent, can be a great way to get them excited to cook. It's also important for everyone to know what burning food smells like so they can react quickly.

The final sense is, of course, taste. Have them taste everything. Have them try the food before and after you cook it (when it's safe to do so) so that they can taste the difference. Have them try a variety of new things and introduce them to new spices.

The brain of someone with ADHD seeks thrilling experiences. By recreating this and engaging their senses, you have a good way to create such an experience for them.

Add Some New Elements To Their Safe Foods

People with ADHD and other brain-diverse conditions tend to have certain safe foods that they are willing to eat, especially on hard days. Now, this step might not be such a good idea on one of those hard days, but on days where they are especially engaged in learning, or if they are really unsure about the cooking process, try this.

If one of their comfort foods is mac and cheese, then try to add some things to it, like meat chunks and vegetables, to make it a balanced meal. Try different brands of mac and cheese too, as some are healthier than others.

Let's say that their comfort food is toast. Toast can be dressed up in so many different ways. Add a nut spread like peanut butter or Nutella. Add an avocado, an egg, or even both. These are just a few examples.

For those that are really hesitant about trying new things, these can help bring them out of their shell one step at a time.

Experimenting Can Be Messy

When it comes to ADHD, we all know that things are rarely clean. What we do see is a lot of mess or organized chaos. If getting them into the kitchen means that there is a mess involved, then so be it. Exploration, especially with food, can do that.

Don't worry; chapter six spends time on cleaning skills.

Mix Foods That Your Child Doesn't Like With Ones That They Do.

We can create a lot of stress for ourselves by trying to get our teens to eat things they don't want. It might come down to a blanket refusal.

This is tricky because they can't avoid certain foods, especially vegetables, forever. So, how do we help with this?

First, remember that we aren't really dealing with children but rather with teens. If we try to be sneaky about adding foods they don't like into their meals, they will notice pretty quickly. Have a conversation with them about the importance and mention that this is a strategy you are going to try. Maybe it's adding some new vegetables into a casserole they like or another way to get them. Ask your teen if they have any suggestions as well because having their input can mean that they are more willing to try the dish.

Flavors

New flavors mean new and thrilling experiences for your ADHD teen. Herbs can add a ton of flavor to a dish, and they are often very healthy. The same is mostly true for spices. Let your teen try them separately and in cooking and have them pick out a few that they really like. You can use this in other dishes later.

Let Them Lead

Most of what we talked about so far has been about introducing them to new foods, senses, and tastes, but most of this is led by you. You aren't going to be there to lead them in cooking when they are older, so at some point, it is important to hand the reins over.

Ask them to make a meal every week and let them have control over it. If you are worried about injury potential, stay close by but gradually withdraw from this the more you see that they are getting it right.

As you go through the steps above, they might have some spices that they want to try, or they may have already thought of some ways to spice up their comfort meal. When we are trying to get them into the kitchen, anything that they can do by themselves is a huge step in the right direction.

Invest In Some Cooking Items That They Might Be Interested In

Cooking stores tend to have a lot of random tools that have a specific purpose. While they might not interest us, your teen might become very invested in them! If there are some tools that seem to pique their interest, get them.

Even in the case of general tools for cooking, a new pan or spatula can be exciting.

Be a Role Model

This last part is one of the most important. If your teen sees you as always cooking and eating healthier and well-balanced meals, they are naturally more likely to join that effort.

Tips For Those Who Are Starting To Cook

Think of a famous chef you know! Gordon Ramsey? Martha Stewart? Do you think that they naturally learned how to cook like that, or was it a process?

It's often a process. Some parts of cooking are going to be straightforward, but there are many mistakes that can be made when your teen is starting out, especially when they have ADHD. The tips I have here for you are great for beginners, but, also, they can really be great for anyone.

Reread the Recipe and Keep It Handy

Today, we can find a lot of the recipes we have just by using our phones. The trouble is that it can be hard to then keep track of where the recipe goes. You are going to need that, especially as you start. Today, most phones come with a bookmark feature. You can use it to create a separate reading list for yourself that includes all of your recipes. Most of them give you a chance to name the bookmark so that you can name it something like the name of the dish rather than keeping the webpage name (which can be really hard to look for).

Another thing to make sure you do before you start the cooking process is to read the recipe all the way through and then reread it. Make sure you know what each step is going to be before you begin. That way, you only have to glance at it during your preparation.

Egg Tip: Ice Or Vinegar

Hard-boiled eggs are relatively easy to cook. They are very difficult to peel, though, unless you try a method to make it easier. One of my favorite methods is putting the eggs in an ice bath immediately after you take them out. By doing this, the egg itself is less attached to the shell and will peel easier. Another common method is adding vinegar to the boiling water.

Finally, how long you let the eggs boil depends on what exactly you are trying to do! If you want softer, gooier eggs, then you can leave them in for as little as four minutes.

Freezing Your Foods

A lot of people today will prepare meals and freeze things for later. If you and your teen are busy, setting time aside at the beginning of the week to cook together and then having these meals ready can be a lifesaver. It does introduce another element: freezing things.

I love fresh fruits and vegetables as much as the next person, but I cannot deny that they tend to go bad before my daughter and I can eat them. Cutting things up and then freezing them for later has been one way we can combat this problem. It helps to do some of the basic parts of preparing them to eat first (cutting the tops off strawberries, slicing carrots, etc.), and then freezing them will make it so that you can just take what you need at the beginning of the day.

Try to seal and get as much air out of the bags as possible when you do this. If the fruit or vegetable is sensitive to spoiling, then having the air in the bag can still cause it to go brown, even if it's frozen.

Another thing you can do if you want to avoid freezer burn is to add cooking oil to the items. This works better with vegetables, but a light coating of something like olive oil can make a difference in how well they do in the freezer. It usually won't affect the taste of the food.

Take Care Of Your Knives

Knife care isn't something that everyone considers to be a part of their cooking routine, but it should be.

Most cooking excerpts will recommend that you sharpen your knives at least once a week (or more, depending on how often they are used). The idea of giving your teen sharper knives when they are just starting out in their cooking journey might seem daunting at first, but there is a good reason for it! They are actually safer than dull knives.

With sharp knives, you get a clean, even slice. Dull knives have a harder time cutting through things, and they will slip a lot more easily and often onto someone's finger (we've all been there). Even if you do manage to cut yourself with a sharp knife, you are likely to realize it sooner!

Experiment With Spice Mixes

Traditional spices always add something unique to food. Spice blends are common, especially in foods from other cultures. If you and your teen are getting bored with the same recipes, don't be afraid to try a spice blend. You can pick one up from a store, but it's more fun to create your own. There are online sources that have lists of what spices are used in different cultures. You can check this out and try some different mixes!

Group Like Steps Together

Here is another great reason to read the recipe first before you do anything else.

A recipe will often have you prepare one part of the meal and then the next. This has you in a cycle of preparing, then cooking, then back to preparing, and then cooking again until you finally combine the ingredients all into a dish. This process can be annoying. It's hard to be efficient.

Grouping your like steps together can cut down on the time you actually spend cooking.

Prepare everything first. If there is something that needs chopped or mixed, get that out of the way so that you can turn to the actual cooking part.

Then, cook everything. A lot of the time, you can reduce the time you spend cooking by half.

Being able to impart some tips that make cooking easier can help you, and your teen start learning how to cook. The next thing I want to share with you is some basic skills to start your teen with!

Basic Skills To Start With When Cooking

Cutting and Chopping

If you've grown up in or around the kitchen, then certain cuts and other things are going to be very familiar to you. For example, what is the difference between chopped and minced food? Also, how do you hold a knife to get what you want out of it?

These skills are important to the success of most recipes.

Degrees of Cooking

How do you like your steak? Do you prefer your bacon crispy? Do you like soft vegetables, or do you prefer them to have a crunch still after they are cooked? Do you like burnt bits of food, or is that not your thing?

How often have you considered questions like this when you are teaching your teen?

Cooking something isn't as simple as it seems. Most foods have to be cooked to a certain point for safety reasons, but after that, it's up to you. Spend some time on this part of cooking, and see if you can find out to which degree your child likes things.

Boiling

It's been a minute since I've left college, but one thing I remember is that a lot of my peers weren't sure of another basic part of cooking: boiling water. Make sure to go over this at least once with your teen and discuss some of the basic foods they can make, including noodles, macaroni and cheese, and hard-boiled eggs.

Cleanliness

I want to highlight this because many people with ADHD understandably struggle with this. In a kitchen, a lack of cleanliness can make you sick. So can cross-contamination. These are absolutely important to teach.

First, there is the concept of basic cleanliness in a kitchen. Teach your child about it. Let them know that by keeping up with cleaning in the kitchen, it keeps away bugs and bacteria.

Cross-contamination is also something you want to talk about. Many of us aren't aware when it happens, but it can make people very sick. Imagine having your teen cook chicken and make a salad for dinner. They cut and start cooking the chicken first because it will take longer, and they can kind of just keep an eye on it while they cut the vegetables.

Not knowing cross-contamination procedures, they immediately switch to chopping vegetables, using the same knife and cutting board without any cleaning procedures done in between. The entire salad has had contact with raw chicken and is now a petri dish of bacteria. Everyone who eats that salad is bound to get sick, and the teen won't realize their mistake until later.

Making sure that your teen knows about cross-contamination in advance can prevent this exact scenario from happening.

Basic Dishes

What are some basic things you can teach your teen to make?

Pasta is one option. Making noodles and throwing on some sauce of their choice creates a great meal.

Another thing is eggs. It's easy to make for breakfast, and you don't have to do a lot of steps.

Sandwiches can be made. And so can many other things. Start by teaching these dishes so that even if cooking isn't their biggest interest, they still have something to take away, and they also have something they can build and grow on.

Food and exercise are so important to our physical health. Our mental health is important too. How do we take care of that?

Chapter Three

Keeping On Top Of Those Emotions

The parents of fourteen-year-old Riley always tried their best with their daughter. She was their joy in life until she had to deal with life's tougher emotions. Riley was prone to outbursts in the form of yelling until she was purple in the face. She would also have explosive panic attacks, and whenever she got stressed, it was always to a point where she would seem to get physically sick. She was finally diagnosed with ADHD, but that just left her parents with more questions than answers. How did something that was about paying attention relate to what she was experiencing now?

They weren't sure what to do. Riley was relying on them to help, and they weren't sure how to provide it or where to start.

If your teen struggles with their emotions, you've probably been in the position of Riley's parents. Children never mean to lose control, but they do. They rely on us to teach them the right ways of handling things so that they can master their feelings. This is true, even when they have ADHD.

Why Does This Happen?

Let's talk a bit about how ADHD affects the brain. Scientists have theories, but they aren't sure about the cause of ADHD. They also aren't 100 percent sure about what exactly in the brain is going wrong, but several cross-examinations and brain scans have led them to some theories.

The leading theory is that the prefrontal cortex in someone with ADHD grows more slowly on average.

The prefrontal cortex is responsible for language, logic, self-control, attention span, and to some extent, emotions.

ADHD is also believed to inhibit one's dopamine flow. Dopamine is a motivational chemical. Without any dopamine in your system, you don't have the motivation to move, even if danger is lurking nearby.

A final impairment that is important to discuss, especially for this chapter, is the concept of flooding. When a typical brain experiences emotions, they experience them like normal, and then the brain switches off. There are remnants of the chemical that created the emotion, but those will soon fade.

An ADHD brain will heavily struggle to have that regulation. It won't turn on and off as we should expect. Instead, the emotional signals keep going until the brain is overwhelmed with the emotional response. This is called flooding, and it's what leads to outbursts, panic attacks, and other intense displays of emotion.

The chemical wires are what's causing meltdowns like Riley's. Once they got ahold of this information, Riley's parents sat down and explained it to her. She felt relieved to understand what was really going on in her brain. This knowledge alone was able to guide her through some of the more mild attacks she'd experienced.

If you notice that your teen does struggle in this area, then give them this knowledge. Knowing what's going on can help them have more control, as logic can help with emotions, and it can help them understand that they aren't bad people; their brain is just being mean.

There are some emotions that our brain does more than others. Unfortunately, these emotions are the ones that even typically brained adults can struggle with.

Stress

Imagine living with ADHD and having to deal with all of the functions it impairs. You're struggling to pay attention at school and work. You're struggling to make sense of what's going on around you. You're struggling with cleaning and maintenance. Everything you're expected to do feels overwhelming to you. It can lead to a huge stress response buildup.

Let's put ourselves in Riley's shoes. She's often very stressed. She has trouble waking up to her alarm. Her room is often messy, so it's hard to gather everything. In class, she has a lot of trouble paying attention, and the teachers like to call on her in order to call her out for this. She has an incredibly difficult time concentrating on homework, and then her parents stress that her room is cleaned and she helps with chores.

For an average person, all of this makes sense, and it's a part of life. For a person with ADHD, as they struggle to do one task after another, it creates stress that they can't escape. Riley's parents get worried because an extra chore or an extra assignment that Riley forgot about can send her over the edge.

Anxiety

Stress is a feeling that is the result of an event. There is a direct cause and effect relationship with stress, but not with anxiety. You can have anxiety about something that has happened, something that might happen, or something that will never happen. There isn't a direct link between the issues at play here.

Stress can cause anxiety, though, and Riley's parents notice it. She tends to get very worked up very quickly. Even in moments when they are watching TV as a family, Riley can't seem to calm down. They've noticed many little habits that Riley seems to have picked up, and it worries them.

Anger

Anger is an emotion that everyone has the right to feel. However, we must be careful in how we express it. Riley has received four detentions in total because she got angry and went off at a teacher. This is very uncharacteristic of their child, who is normally very sweet and well-tempered.

Riley has also gone off on them multiple times. Physically, she will only throw herself to the ground or physically hit her head against the wall, but her parents have heard horror stories about children who broke walls or whose parents had to press charges.

Anger is one of the biggest emotions that flood the system of an ADHD person. It will keep going until they fly into a rage. Even as Riley has calmed down in the past, she still has felt overwhelmingly angry. She just didn't have the energy to continue the outburst.

In order for our children to be successful, they need to be able to control these emotions. Give them a chance to work through it if you can. Help them through different strategies so that they can hopefully do it on their own soon.

Strategies For Dealing With These Emotions

Stress

If we have just the right amount of stress, then we are motivated to focus and get our work done. But, when we get to the point where we have too much stress, the situation starts to get out of control. When you have ADHD, and your brain is capable of flooding, then it becomes harder to walk that line.

If your teen keeps trying to get their work done but finds that they keep struggling to, suggest things like listening to music. Have them create a to-do list or keep a planner. Having one of these makes it easier to make sure that things are getting done. Fewer things slip through the cracks, you don't have to do the tracking with your brain, and it's satisfying to cross something off after it has been completed.

Another thing that can help is to only focus on one thing and get that done before moving on. Trying to do multiple tasks at once isn't going to help. That may actually hurt you since the time it takes to switch between tasks is going to take up more time than it would to focus on one task. The exception to this is when you are stuck and can't move forward.

For example, if your teen is struggling with their math homework and no matter what they do, they just can't figure it out and seem to be close to tears, then it might be time to move on to another subject. Going back to their math homework with a fresh pair of eyes can make a difference in their interpretation.

Another thing to do is make sure to focus on one task at a time. Teens often get a ton of homework, and it can be overwhelming to think about how much you might have to do. Looking at one piece at a time instead of the big picture can help you focus on what needs to be done without getting stressed.

Another tip is taking breaks. Make sure that this is a part of your teen's routine if they have several hours of homework to do. Have them take a five-minute breathing break after they get through a subject. Have them get through a few subjects and then go and exercise. Things like this can help the stress response relax and prevent flooding.

Teach your teen to speak up for themself and offer them a safe space to do that. If they feel like they can't tell others when they are overwhelmed, then they won't. Eventually, their silence will lead to a meltdown.

Communication is key. Speaking up when they need to is part of it. Another part is just ensuring that communication is something your child is good at, and they should be able to communicate with you about what they need from you. They should be able to communicate with their teachers if there is something that they are struggling with. Being able to speak your needs can help to reduce stress significantly.

Problem-solving abilities are going to be another preventative factor in stress management. By being able to sit there and figure out the answer to the problem at hand, your teen is going to find themselves less stressed. For example, the problem could easily be that there is an overwhelming amount of homework for the weekend. Your teen may solve a problem that involves tackling his math homework Friday night, his English and history papers on Saturday, and his science on Sunday. Everything gets done with a solution that your teen was able to think through.

When all of these don't work, have some things ready that just naturally reduce stress. Get your favorite snack. Meditate (which we will talk about more later in this chapter).

If there is something that doesn't have to be dealt with, then don't. It's not imperative that they do the extra credit if there are other assignments. If they have a free period before math class and know that they can get it done, move on.

Finally, give them as much control as possible in their lives. They are going to be an adult soon, so being able to have control over their life while they still have your guidance close by is going to give them a chance to experiment safely. Let them choose their classes and electives, so long as they are meeting graduation requirements.

On a day-to-day basis, let them choose where they want to do their homework. It could be inside, outside, in their room, or at the kitchen table. Letting them have the option of sitting wherever they like can alleviate some of the stress they might face.

Stress often has a direct cause, so many of its strategies are aimed at reducing the magnitude of the cost so that the person can better deal with it later. Our next topic is anxiety, which is a bit different.

Anxiety

As we talked about earlier, anxiety isn't directly related to a cause, so managing the cause might not help how a person is feeling—because of this, trying to work on the direct cause might make it worse because your teen is focusing on the problem even more.

Sadly, we can't avoid most causes of anxiety. Things like going to school are common triggers. What we can do is work on the thoughts and feelings surrounding anxiety.

Create a brainstorm for anxiety and its causes. Talk to your teen about the specifics of their anxiety and see what can be done to ease it. Let's continue to use school as an example.

Your teen has anxiety about going to school. When does it start? Where are they? They might answer that it starts as soon as they get up, when they start the commute to school, or when they first walk into the building. Ask them if there are any specific triggers. Is it the tone of voice of a teacher or seeing certain people? Have these people done anything to warrant the anxiety (in which case, what steps can be taken to make sure it doesn't happen again)? Is it just there? What about certain activities or classes at school?

School is a broad thing to be anxious about, but if you and your teen can narrow down the specific reason it's happening, it can make the rest of school more bearable, and it can put more focus on a solution, which is the thing to ask about next.

What happens when they get to school, and they run into the trigger, or the feeling starts to rise? What are some things they can do?

Having a thought-out strategy can ease some of those feelings. Our thoughts are much easier to control, and if we get a good handle on them, it can ease our feelings.

If that doesn't seem to be working, ask your teen about potential distractors. Can they listen to music, doodle, read, or find a simple game that they like that can help?

Logic won't always work on anxiety, but redirections and distractions can have a powerful effect. A final thing for your teens to remember is that, much like ADHD, anxiety can feel like it's a part of your personality. It's not. Yes, you might struggle with it, and it can have a big impact on your everyday life, but that doesn't mean that it's who you are.

It can be tempting for you to step in when their anxiety is high and just fix everything for them. With anxiety being such a toxic emotion, this instinct is natural. Sadly, it will do more harm than good to do this. By stepping in and taking them away from the anxiousness, they are losing a chance to deal with their own problems. Never facing the issues giving them anxiety can make their anxiety worse in the long run. People who suffer from anxiety often find that it never quite leaves them, but they do find ways to manage it the more they interact with it. For your soon-to-be adult, this skill is necessary.

Instead, create a safe space. Provide relief for the anxiety in other ways by letting them come to a place where they don't have to feel it. Give them an opportunity to cool down and breathe. When they are struggling, be someone with who they can talk about their struggles. You don't have to have answers for them, but by being there and being a safe person, their body and mind will give them a break.

One thing to keep in mind is that not every teen will see their home as their safe space. This isn't always because of a lack of sameness in the home. It's often because there is just another area that is familiar and safe to them. It could be a library or a coffee shop. It could be a park or a skating rink. It could be the beach or a pool. Whatever the case might be, that's a safe place. Make time as often as possible for them to visit it, especially after they have to deal with high anxiety situations.

When your teen feels like their anxiety has locked them into a box of sorts and they can't move forward, talk to them about small, incremental goals that they can do that can slowly help them be able to function. It could be that they are terrified to do their homework because they think they are going to fail. A goal for this might be to forget about doing it well. Just finish the assignments and turn them in. Any grade is better than a zero.

In these cases, they also try to steer their mind in a different direction. They already know what's going to happen if their anxieties come true. They've likely spent hours agonizing over it. Ask them what's going to happen if the good outcome is met? What if your kid gets a good grade? Ask them to describe what would happen then.

You might notice a theme that, in dealing with anxiety, there isn't much problem-solving. Instead, it's made to be more about managing feelings. Anxiety is a feeling that needs to be managed, and solving problems won't do the trick. Instead, we focus on how to bring our anxiety levels back down so that we can effectively live life. That's how working with anxiety goes. We can't defeat it as we can with stress, so we instead learn to overcome it.

Anger

It's not uncommon for children with ADHD to have anger issues. Many children with ADHD are in trouble because their anger leads them to act out. As children, trouble looks like a note home to the parents, detention, or suspension.

As adults, losing control of our anger can mean the loss of a job, a loved one, and even criminal charges. Anger cannot go unchecked. It's an emotion that we must deal with and respond appropriately to.

As our children enter their teen years, they have to deal with hormones on top of the flooding that their brain might already experience, creating the perfect conditions for a full tornado of rage.

It's important for teens to have strategies that manage this anger so that they can still live and not have to worry about blowing up at someone.

One such strategy is exercise. A lot of strong emotions can fuel a workout or be channeled into sports. Exercising can help by putting that rage into physical use. Making sufficient time for exercise can help the brain be more at ease as well, instead of keeping these feelings all pent up.

Coach your teen not only by making exercise a regular habit but also by understanding that if they need to take a break during something and walk off some of that energy, they should be able to do so. It is better to take that breather than to go into a rage. Conditions like ADHD are covered by ADA laws, and you can get a doctor to put this in a 504 plan. This means that even if they are at school or work, they should be able to walk away when they need to, and there shouldn't be any consequences (so long as this isn't abused).

Another thing to do is to help your teen work on vocalizing their feelings instead of acting on them. When they start to run into overwhelming anger, which is often due to flooding, work on statements such as "I'm getting very angry right now" or "this anger is too much for me, and I need to step out." The vocalization alone can sometimes help, and it gives the people around them a heads up.

Another thing to do is look into the use of electronics. This one is hard because electronics are such a huge part of our lives, and at this point, your teen probably needs them to complete daily functions. That being said, they've been tied to angry outbursts, as well as other emotional issues such as depression. Try to have your teen spend a certain amount of time away from a screen. This can be reading a book, cooking, eating, or doing something outside. The break can have a powerful effect on the mind, and it can help calm any brewing outbursts.

Another thing to do is to make sure that your child is in touch with their feelings. How can they know that they need to step out and take a walk or that they need to vocalize their feelings if they can't really feel what's about to happen until it's too late? If they are able to identify their emotions as a signal ahead of time, then they can dive into reduction tactics.

Keep in mind, as you prepare your teen for the adult world, that there are some situations that are causing anger that they won't have to deal with. A curfew is one example. When there are issues like these, and they are causing anger, then it's time to sit down and discuss the issue. Try to compromise and let them have a chance to talk about what's going on. If there isn't a need for an issue, but they are getting angry over it, then it may be a good idea to let it go. Your teen will soon find out on their own why it's important to go to bed at a certain time. The misbehavior due to these issues is more attributable to ADHD than anything that they are intentionally doing.

Have your teen keep a record of their emotions and anything they have done that helps them get through negative emotions. This gives them some responsibility for their emotions and how to calm them down.

The final thing that you can do for anger is just to make sure that your teen has a space to talk through it. Anger is an emotion that shouldn't be acted on, as it can destroy great things. It is an emotion that we need to deal with, and discussion can be a huge part of that.

Emotions are tough. Adults with a typical brain will struggle with keeping their emotions in check.

Imagine having ADHD and having to deal with flooding when it comes to stress, anxiety, or anger. It's a difficult thing that is going to require some extra strategies to deal with. At the end of the day, remind your teen that they are not their emotions and that it's going to be challenging, but they have strategies to get through it!

The same is going to be true for our next chapter. Time management is something that everyone struggles with, but this is often more the case for those with ADHD. What additional strategies can help them?

Chapter Four

Time Management and Organization Skills

Let's take a moment to consider the stereotypical ADHD adult. They wake up late because they "forgot" to set their alarm. They rush around, and everything around them is a mess. They can't find anything, and there is chaos and clutter everywhere.

They leave the house looking like a cluttered mess and forget half the things they were supposed to bring with them.

While they work, they are constantly distracted by other things. They seem to always be focused on other things, and they aren't as competent. There is no organization in their life; they are always late and have terrible time management. A company cannot discriminate by not hiring someone with ADHD, but because of these stereotypes, they may try to avoid it at all costs.

It's easy for someone with ADHD to fall into this stereotype, but there are so many strategies that help prevent it, so how do we help your teen?

The younger you can start these strategies, the more ingrained the habits will be.

Time Management

There are so many things that we need to get done each day. Those things don't often include timed obligations such as appointments, work schedules, and the need to be in class on time.

The ADHD brain doesn't naturally keep a schedule, so it's essential to make use of helpful outside resources to do this.

Have Something Near You At All Times That Can Give You the Time

This one is kind of easy as we all seem to have our phones on us constantly. That is perfect if that can give your teen the time at all hours. But they might not always have it on them, not make a habit of glancing at it, or they might not be allowed to look at it (many high schools still ban the use of phones in school).

Watches are another great alternative. Having a clock in their room can be beneficial for them as well. Having time constantly near them can help them with punctuality, and it can also provide a way to time tasks. If your child has a day where they aren't really interested in doing anything, then setting appropriate timers for tasks can help. Conversely, if they have a day where they are hyper-focused on something, but you are worried that it will absorb too much of their day, then you can have them set timers for that too.

If, even with a clock, your teen still struggles with punctuality, have them set alarms for each step of the day. At 6 a.m., they get up and make their bed. At 6:15, they have breakfast. At 6:45, they get dressed and ready for the day. This pattern continues until they have their alarm for when it's time to leave. If you worry that they will still be late, try adding five to ten additional minutes into their routine somewhere. It could be that they get up ten minutes earlier than they need to or that you think of the event you're trying to go to as being ten minutes earlier than it is scheduled (and you write it down as such). This way, there is a little bit of lax time for them to play with, and they have a good chance of getting there on time.

Create A Timesheet

It can be easy for anyone to forget all of the little details in a day, especially when a person has ADHD.

Think of a school schedule and all the activities and homework following it. Things are bound to slip through the cracks, especially if it's the start of a semester and the schedule is new.

Writing out a timesheet can be helpful for your teen. They can try a simple one that tells them where their classes are and where they need to be, or they can make it highly detailed. Some timesheets include a write-out of their morning routine, their commute, each detail of their class schedule, their commute to an afterschool activity, the activity itself, a commute home, time divided out for studying in each subject, followed by dinner, and their night routine.

Does that sound like a lot? Yes, it probably does, but it can be helpful to those who need that detail.

Have Them Do Work In Their Peak Productivity Time

In high school, this is a little harder because the expectations of a schedule are so rigid, but introducing this concept now will help them in their college or career path.

There is a theory that everyone has a time where they are most productive. For some, it's the crack of dawn. For others, this time might be mid-morning. For others still, this might be afternoon, evening, late at night, etc. Whatever this time is, the brain is doing its best work.

Let them as much as possible if there is any way for your teen to do their homework in these times. If their peak time is the early morning, let them save their most time-intensive subject for that time. If it's late at night, let them go to sleep later, so long as they can at least make sure that they are getting enough sleep.

If your teen goes to college, then they can build their class schedule in such a way that it lets them do their homework in their peak time.

Leave Free Time In Their Day To Day Schedule

What happens to you and your brain if you constantly have to think about a long list of tasks or meetings you need to complete in a day? We all have a few days where things are like this, but if this becomes the case every single day, it can be awful and very stressful. This will also be true for your teen.

School already provides a rigid structure that takes up most of their day. If they have a club, a sport, and several other activities after that, even more of their day is gone to schedule. When it gets so full that they feel like they cannot have a break, then we have stress.

Ask your teen about their schedule. Is it too much? Or do they enjoy it? As adults, they will have the power to put whatever they want into their day, and teaching them as teens that they don't have to pack their schedule with things if they don't want to can help them be more relaxed and well-adjusted as adults.

Prioritize Your Day

When we are teens, schooling will be a top priority. As adults, it's work and sometimes parenting. After this, there are other things that we consider a priority. When your teen adds their priority items to their schedule, make sure that it's in a way where they are made a priority. Start that habit now, so it's easier when they are adults. Some other priorities that might be considered include homework (maybe some subjects take priority over others depending on time, grades, or enjoyment), activities they love, or other obligations.

Get Enough Sleep

Speaking of priorities, let's talk about sleep. Sleep is essential to everyone's ability to function.

As we go through our day-to-day lives, we use the power that our brain has stored. Neurons will degenerate into providing the continuing ability to function. When we sleep, those neurons will regenerate, giving us renewed power for the next day.

When we don't get enough sleep, our neurons won't fully regenerate, and it forces our brain to essentially use a backup generator. Now, we can run on this backup generator for several days before our brain reaches for the neurons that are essential to our function. Still, with each day that the backup generator is running, we are losing our ability to function. The good news is that one good night of sleep erases two or three bad nights, but that feeling of your brain lagging will happen with just one night with poor or too little sleep.

Your child needs to understand the necessity of sleep and share this knowledge so that they know to prioritize it throughout their lives.

Then, work on a sleep schedule with them. Figure out what their body needs. While eight hours is recommended nationally, many people do fine with as little as six, and others need 10.

Once your teen is sure about what their body needs, make it into a habit that goes into their schedule.

Make Sure That the Schedule Is Enjoyable

If they don't like it, then they won't follow it. Yes, there will be things on there that they don't like, but if the entire schedule is just full of stuff like that, why would they try to follow it?

When the schedule is made, set some parameters (getting enough sleep and time for school) and then let them build it and make sure they will enjoy it. That's the only way the schedule will work.

Try Not To Make Too Many Changes

We want to create a schedule that is easy to follow, not one that's confusing.

Now, as the schedule starts out, there might be some changes as you realize that a commute takes longer (maybe you didn't factor in the time it took to walk to class) or that a specific part of the schedule does better at a different time of day, or something else, but once the kinks are ironed out, make the schedule consistent, with as little change as possible.

Choose the Time Frame You Are Scheduling

Some people do the same thing every day, and others have schedules where they do different things each day of the week. When your teen is making their schedule, have them account for this. Monday and Tuesday might need different schedules.

Try to make each schedule as similar as possible so that they are easy to follow, but make sure that everything is accounted for.

Have A Schedule For the Weekends Too

This one will be a little annoying, but it's essential. A weekend schedule will be looser and probably include lots of free time, but if there are obligations to attend to, even if it's just cleaning your house, make sure they make it onto that schedule.

To-Do List

This tip is stressed in just about every organization and time management topic, which may be annoying, but it's also a testament to just how powerful this is. A to-do list makes it so nothing slips through the cracks, and there are several ways to build one.

First, encourage your teen to keep the syllabus that they get at the beginning of the year. These often contain a course schedule, and information about papers and exams will be on it. If you and your teen want to be on top of things, designate a time to sit down and plan the week. Using a daily or weekly planner can help. Take the time to assign assignments to certain days. Doing this means that the amount of homework is much less overwhelming, and you know when each thing will get done. You can also prepare for tests you know are coming up or big projects that are due in a few weeks.

To help your teen get excited about this and make it visual and easy to follow, use colored pens or highlighters to designate which subject the assignment is for.

If your teen isn't big on planning their week out, a simple to-do list with the assignments they get can help them at least keep track of everything and make sure it gets done.

From here, it helps to take it one step further. At the beginning of each day, sit down and write out a daily to-do list. If your teen has planned their week in advance, then this will be an easy step for them. If your teen adheres to a weekly to-do list, this step will be beneficial to them. This is a time when they can write down assignments, meetings, chores, and anything else they need to get done during the day. Even if your child already keeps a weekly or daily planner, this extra step can help them be prepared for the day as they go into it and stops them from looking at their planner in surprise later.

Pay Attention To How, When, and How Long They Procrastinate

Procrastination is a common pitfall for those who suffer from ADHD. Except, it doesn't happen in the same way it would in a typical brain. First of all, remember that ADHD often relates to functions commonly found in the frontal lobe. One of the things that the frontal lobe is in control of is our attention span. If an activity isn't interesting to us, we don't really want to pay attention, but we might be able to force ourselves to do so. Our teens have even less of a capacity to do that than we do.

Now the flip side is hyperfocus, where your teen is engaged and uninterruptible. They enjoy it, and their brain is almost making too much of the chemical they need. Unless it's interfering with their schedule, this likely isn't what you're worried about.

There is also an issue of dopamine, or the motivation chemical, not being produced as much.

When your teen is procrastinating, have them track it. First of all, how are they procrastinating? Are they taking a long time to prepare for the task? Are they looking at social media? Watching Netflix? Napping (when it isn't needed)?

Next, think about when they are procrastinating. Is it before homework? A particular subject in homework? Is it chores?

Finally, how long do they spend procrastinating? And how big of an effect does it have on their performance? If the effect is minimal to none, then it may be best to leave it alone.

If the effect on their performance is a big one, then something does need to be addressed. These details can also tell you other things.

Procrastination is currently creating more dopamine than doing the work. Is there a way to adjust that?

First, let's look at how your teen might procrastinate. Is it that they take too long to get ready to do the task? Maybe they sit down to study, work for five minutes, and then decide they need a snack. They get up, go get one, and sit back down. After another five minutes, the snack makes them thirsty. They get up, get water, and sit back down. They might decide you need more pencils or paper, coffee, tea, another snack, or something else. Whatever it is, the end result is that they have spent more time getting ready to do the task and less time on the task itself.

To solve this, when you notice that they are having an awful time with this issue, have them write down everything they had to get up and get. The next time, get everything first so that there isn't anything to grab later.

What if their method of procrastination is going on their phone for social media or to watch a movie? Set break times for those apps (most phones will let you lock them for a certain length of time). You can also try focus apps or Pomodoro methods to help.

Now, when do they procrastinate? Is it before chores? See if there are certain chores that don't engage them. We will have some tips for those in the next section.

Is it homework? Focus apps can help with this, as can app restrictions and limits. What if it's just a particular subject? If they are procrastinating because they really don't want to touch the material of their least favorite class, have them work on a different one. Sometimes, all we need is to get started. Other times, well, at least the other work is getting done.

Add Something To Mundane Tasks To Make It Interesting

If the tasks are chore related, let them listen to music or a podcast. Let them watch something if it doesn't affect the task. These can increase your child's attention span and ability to get them done.

Now, if that doesn't work, then we need to move to the next step, which is to make everything into a game.

Now, when we talk about the brain having issues with motivation, we are solely speaking about intrinsic motivation. Extrinsic motivation, where the person is motivated by reward, is still able to be used to help you.

The satisfaction of being timed and beating a goal might be enough. If not, try candy, an allowance, privileges that they don't usually get, or a chance to go to an event you know they want to attend. This extrinsic motivation can often bridge the gap.

Try Not To Look Over Their Shoulder

When your teen leaves the nest, they aren't going to have you there to remind them of all of the little things that help them, and they are likely to drop several habits.

Furthermore, if you push ideas onto them, it may make the situation worse. It's not likely that all of these ideas are going to be a perfect fit, and your teen is likely to resist some of them. Move on to the next. Let them figure out their system. This is the best way to make it stick into adulthood.

Goal Setting

Goal setting is the final time management habit that I want to discuss today. First of all, by setting goals, your teen has a reason to think of when her brain tries to resist her.

Second, by talking about goals with another person (you), your teen learns the importance of goal setting and how it can help hold them accountable for meeting those goals.

Finally, goals measure progress. By making progress, we know that we are getting somewhere. When your teen is having a bad day and wants to give up, use her progress toward her goals as motivation.

Time management isn't something your teen struggles with alone. Many people, whether they have ADHD or not, will find challenges in time management. ADHD simply presents some unique challenges to time management. These tips can help navigate some of the challenges.

Another major challenge that ADHD creates for kids is that of organization.

Organization Tips For ADHD

People with ADHD are stereotypically messy. If you think about some of the challenges that they face, it probably isn't surprising to learn that there is some truth to this.

There are issues with focus and motivation, so when it's all combined, things can get... interesting.

How do we navigate these key issues?

After much searching, there turned out to be several tips on how to manage this properly.

Limit How Long You Spend On Decisions

Have you ever noticed that your teen always has a hard time making up their mind? That is a part of executive dysfunction. It's one of the bigger struggles for ADHD. Schedules, to-do lists, and more things where decisions are made ahead of time can really help when it comes to these problems.

When that's not possible, try setting timers. This can be stressful at first, but your teen will likely eventually slide into this.

Try Not To Do Too Much

We already talked about not jamming a schedule so full that there isn't room to just sit down and breathe. Now, we are going to talk about overcommitment. When getting your teen to organize, they might overcommit to a task and either spend way more hours on it than they should, or they might run out of motivation halfway through.

When you start teaching them this concept, guide them. When they talk about big projects, see if you can talk them into scaling back or planning to do this in stages. Show enthusiasm, but also remind them that this might not be the perfect fix they are hoping for.

Work Together

This doesn't mean that you and your teen are working together on their homework.

Have you ever gone to a coffee shop or library to get some work done? I certainly have, and I've been tempted to look on my phone while I'm there. But unlike when I'm at home, and no one is watching, I don't do that. There is something about having others who are there and working with you that just makes everything so much more engaged. Use an effect like this to your advantage. Sit with your teen and work. You could be doing work, creating a budget, looking at new recipes, or whatever you need to get done that will help your teen. If you are working, they are more likely to naturally do so too!

Keep Everything Bright And Visual

I cannot stress this enough. Have things that are visual. Bright, visible things are much easier for the brain to take in. When your child has ADHD, it makes a difference. Label things. Have them label things.

Color code stuff. Do whatever you need to do to help your child make it visual in a way that they can work with.

Help Your Teen Fight Clutter

There are so many things out there that we can buy that we will never use again. These just take up space and become a mess that we have to deal with.

Your teen might have spending money of their own. They might find that when they see it in a store, it's cute. So, they take it home, they put it on their desk or on a shelf, and it's never handled again. Despite this, they will fight to keep it until the day they die.

This is a step that your teen will need either your assistance or the assistance of others.

First of all, when they are buying things, don't let them shop alone if you can help it. If you aren't there, let their friends be their moral compass. When they consider buying something, ask them what use it is going to have. If they don't seem to have an answer, try to convince them to put it back.

Now, when they are trying to clean and declutter their room, either be there or have someone else that they are close with to be there. Be the logic to their emotion if they try to justify the item's place.

Manage The Number Of Projects Your Teen Is Trying To Do

Hyperfocus and a sudden stop in motivation can lead to massive projects that are halfway finished. Obviously, this is a struggle. They take up time and space, but it doesn't feel like there is anything you can do.

Try to guide them to two to three projects at a time. Have them manage them. It can help them get control and finish things without also feeling overwhelmed by the projects they already have.

Use A Timer To Organize

A big mess isn't going to be easy to clean, and spending time on it can feel exhausting. When you have ADHD, and all you see is a big mess, it can be overwhelming to think about cleaning it. Your teen might procrastinate as a result of this.

A popular way that people have fought this is by setting a ten to fifteen-minute timer every day and using that timer as the time they have to clean and declutter. If their room or other spaces are really messy, 15 minutes may admittedly not seem like enough, but if it's done every day, they will catch up to the mess, and it helps to prevent future messes from getting out of control.

Have a Centralized Spot For Things You Need To Leave The House

This has the power to benefit everyone in your home, and it's a great thing for your teen later.

Have some command hooks, a basket, or another method for everyone to store their keys, wallet, mask, and anything else they might need to leave the house.

Find Some Different Organization Methods Online With Your Teen

This last tip is for if you and your teen are really struggling to come up with a system of organization. If no matter what you do, you can't seem to figure out one that works for your house, then it's time to look online. Do this with your teen and try to help get them excited for a step like this. It can help them get organized now and understand how to look for resources when they need them in the future.

Organization and time management are not innate skills in any of us, but they can be learned. It can be hard to pick up when ADHD is involved, but implementing some extra strategies can really help!

Chapter Five

Money Management

At the beginning of her adult life, Lisa took out several credit cards and a few loans. She spent it with little thought and no budget.

By the time she was 25, it had caught up to her. She nearly had to move back in with her parents because she didn't have enough money for rent or other expenses. At this point, she was able to save herself and pull herself back up on her feet. She got married and had her son, and she'd been able to give her son a life with all his necessities met and several other luxuries, like vacations, sports, new clothes, and a car. Her son James hasn't had to worry about money, and she worries that he will make the same mistakes.

Her husband has told her not to worry. It's just a part of James' ADHD, and he will grow out of it. Lisa still worries.

She needs to teach James the basics of money management, and soon. Otherwise, he might head down the same path, and with his ADHD, he might not realize it until it's too late.

Understandably, you probably want your teen to avoid the same fate. You don't want them going down a path where they overspend, go into debt, and get themselves into a mess that they can't get out of.

A lot of it will come from putting the responsibility in their hands early, which we are going to start talking about.

Get Them The Proper Supplies

What does your teen need to manage money?

First, they are going to need a way to keep a budget, which can be a physical checkbook, a notebook, an excel spreadsheet, or really whatever is easiest for your teen. In addition to this, they are going to want a calculator and possibly some writing utensils. If your teen primarily earns cash, then they either will need a bank account for cash storage or a system to budget the cash at home. Some money experts recommend using cash envelopes for budgeting. The pro is that you have a visual representation of how much money you have. On the other hand, it does create some risk.

Let Them Get A Job

In order to learn how to handle money, they have to be able to earn it. A part-time job can be worked around school and can be an excellent outlet for physical exercise. Plus, they can get something to put on their resume.

Having a job is something we all have to do for most of our lives. There are benefits to learning how to handle a job as a teenager, especially as someone who has ADHD. There are many customer service jobs that involve a lot of tasks and a lot of business, and someone with ADHD, whose brain is constantly moving to the next thing, can find a good groove here.

A job will let them earn money that you can use to teach them. Many of the tips here are dependent on them having some sort of stream of income, whether it's a physical job, online work, or under-the-table work.

Guide Your Teen In Creating Their First Budget

Creating your first budget can be overwhelming, regardless of how your brain might be composed. It's always a good idea to be there that first time so that you can explain some of the things that need to be done.

First of all, how do you decide when to budget? People who are salaried or know in advance how much money they are going to make have the advantage of planning in advance. Your teen might not have that, especially if they have a changing schedule. If this is the case, get them into the habit of budgeting no more than 48 hours later. When you get your kid to budget, start with their needs. Do they have any bills that need to be paid? What about clothes? School supplies? School lunches? As they get older, they might want certain clothes or supplies, and they might want to get lunch off-campus. These would be great uses for their budget.

Next, consider the wants they might have. Some things, like certain clothes, are technically a need and a want and can be budgeted for before this category. Their wants might be things like a new gaming system, a new phone, or something else that they are looking to get.

There is also the matter of saving for bigger purchases like a car or college if that's the route they want to go. If you aren't sure what money is going to be brought in, always set aside the proper amounts for bills and then go into the other items and assign them a certain percentage of the budget.

After you have sat down and discussed this, set aside some time to go over it with them in the future and hold them accountable to stick to it, most banking is online now, so it's much easier to be aware of what's going in and out.

Talk To Them About Long-Term Goals

Like we talked about above in the budgeting sections, there are going to be long-term saving goals for your child that are going to help them in the long run.

Most children want a car as they hit their legal driving age. While some families can afford to help out with this, some can't. If your teen is starting to make money, then start talking to them about this as one of their long-term goals.

Another potential long-term goal is college. Today, we do live in a place where a college degree isn't always needed, but for many, it is the route they want to take. If your teen is interested in college, this is another thing to be saving for.

Saving doesn't automatically sound appealing, and we have to remember that a part of ADHD is impulsive decisions, which can be made with money.

First, the goals should be reasonable and set by your teen more than they are set by you.

Next, make sure that your teen has a visible way to track their budget. The money envelope system is helpful for this because money for spending is separate from saving. There are just two issues. One issue is a security concern of having all cash assets. The other is that a lot of shopping is done online.

If your teen isn't interested in making online purchases, and you know that the safety of their money is practically guaranteed, then this might be a viable option.

Another great way to make their spending visual is to install their bank app on their phone. It can track money and often holds spending charts. If you think it will help, you can all draw these charts onto a dry-erase board.

The final thing you can do is start a savings account for your teen. This separates the money that they are supposed to save so that it can't be easily spent.

Another component of this is to make the goals visual.

If your teen is looking forward to a car, start researching cars that they might want. Do some research online with your teen so that they learn some sales terminology, get an idea of what features they might want, and they know what to look for in cars. Used cars are often the way to go in terms of a first car, but to get one also requires extra knowledge (including how to tell if you are being scammed). All of this research can help make your teen excited to reach their goal. As they save, help them envision their dream car. It makes the goal real and appealing.

Another common long-term saving goal is college. A lot of the steps are going to be the same, and they are important for more reasons than just budgeting. First, what major is your child interested in heading toward? Most colleges don't carry every single major that there is.

Next, do they want to be in the state or out of state? Do they understand the cost difference between the two? Finally, what schools specifically are they looking at? Many schools will list information about their cost of attendance online, and your teen can easily view this information. While college itself is scary, campus and dorm room pictures, researching the town they might go to, and gaining knowledge on their program can get them excited and help motivate them to save.

The same formula works best with most long-term goals. Researching the goal can help your teen get excited about it, and it can also help them get motivated to save up so that it can happen. Long-term goals will be, in some way, a part of our budget forever, so we need to start thinking about them at a younger age.

Explaining Debt

Does your teen understand what it means to be in debt? Do they know what kind of consequences are associated with it?

Loans are a tool, and this tool has to be used wisely. If we aren't wise about our loan decisions, then we end up in deep trouble. The impulsive nature of ADHD might create a situation where your child readily uses their card and doesn't think about the consequence of doing so. We don't want them to leave our house without the knowledge of how to properly make decisions about loans and debt.

First, let's talk about loans. Loans are sometimes just a part of life. People get loans for a car, college, and houses all of the time. The tricky part about loans isn't the loans themselves but the interest. In the long run, you pay more money over time.

A trick that I have found helpful when teaching about money and loans is to ask, "will this help you advance in your life?"

A car loan probably will if it helps you get a good car that outlives the loan. What about student loans? They are a pain, but they will absolutely help you advance. Home loans? Yup, those too!

Now, what about a loan for the latest phone? Probably not, unless your teen is making money through their device (after all, many phones have the capacity of a professional camera). Purchases that are for fun should probably not be made into a loan.

Again, this is a part of fighting the natural impulsive tendencies of ADHD.

Next, let's talk about credit cards. Again, they are a great tool, but they have to be used wisely.

Teach your teen that they should expect to pay the balance in full each month, as that is what keeps them out of debt and helps build their credit score. Also, some credit cards are better than others, and it's helpful to understand that too.

When this knowledge fails to help them, then they experience natural consequences, which we will talk about at the end of this chapter.

Subscriptions

Subscriptions have a unique teaching power that you can't really find anywhere else at that young age.

Bills are a part of adult life, but when we are teenagers, there aren't many bills to consider. How do we then teach the concept of bills?

One way to do this is through subscription services. These come in many forms. There are things like Netflix and other streaming services. There are also things like subscription boxes. If your family already pays for streaming services, then subscription boxes may be the way to go.

The joy of a subscription box is that it can be catered to things that your child is interested in. This could be books, art, cooking, or other hobbies. This gives them something visual to look forward to every month while creating a bill for them to manage. You can get a couple of boxes to provide them with the experience of having a couple of bills, but keep in mind that this might create a problem of too much clutter.

If your teen struggles to budget for this appropriately, then we move into the phase of natural consequences.

Natural Consequences

Now that I have brought them up a few times, it's time to talk about what natural consequences mean. Money is great when it comes to this.

There are many times in our children's lives when we don't need to rely on methods of discipline or punishment. Their actions have natural consequences or something that logically follows their action. For children with ADHD, this is actually an excellent way for them to learn, as a lot of punishment and discipline do not have the intended effect. Instead, a child with ADHD is likely to focus on what happened or the negative of the punishment or discipline method, and the actual lesson will be lost. On the other hand, a natural consequence creates a cause-and-effect relationship that won't be forgotten so easily.

How does this work with loans? Your child now has to pay these back, and they lose more money each month to bills. If they don't pay them back, then it hurts their credit score, and it could get them in legal trouble. Plus, if they buy something like a new phone, and don't pay the loan back, then they often get another loan for the next new phone.

What about credit card statements? Same thing. If your child uses their card too much, they will eventually hit their limit, and if it's not paid on time, the card will get declined. It won't come back until your teen has paid what they need to pay.

What about subscriptions and streaming services? What happens if your child doesn't save the way that they are supposed to, and they end up not having enough to cover the subscription? Most subscriptions can be paused for a month.

These are all natural consequences of their actions. If they use money improperly, then they have to face the fact that they now need to make sacrifices and cuts. They lose out on things that they enjoy.

I understand that it might be really tempting to step in and save them, but you aren't doing them any favors. They can dig themselves out of this hole, and it's best that they are learning now and not later.

A lot of success is found when support and guidance are offered, but not assistance.

Money is something that many people feel is too tight today and a lot of people have to create budgets. Your teen is going to be no exception.

Understanding the basics now can prepare them for the future, which is often less kind.

It's going to feel interesting when your teen talks about getting loans or wanting a car, but these things are normal and great learning opportunities.

Chapter Six

At Home Maintenance

As adults, we can technically call a repairman for anything we want. We can also hire a cleaning agency or housekeeper. We can hire someone to organize our money and our documents. There is a service for pretty much every adult need you could have. The trouble? That's expensive. Not only is it cheaper, but it is much faster to do it yourself.

Now, what about your teen? They have ADHD. These things are going to be tough, right? They have such a hard time taking care of things at home; how are they going to fare when they get their own place?

While I think this is a valid concern, I don't want you to worry.

To illustrate my point, I want you to meet Emma. Today, Emma is a stay-at-home mom. She cooks, cleans, balances the budget, sorts documents, and with the help of her husband, she keeps a household for four children (two of which have ADHD) afloat.

If you met her in college, you would be surprised. Emma left home with no ideas about things like how to do laundry or make a pot of noodles. Her parents always thought of her as scatterbrained, and though her mom made a few small attempts to teach Emma some of these skills, she always gave up in the end. This didn't benefit Emma, who struggled a lot at first and had to ask her roommates for a lot of help.

At the age of 22, a year away from graduation, Emma was finally diagnosed with ADHD. She now understood why her parents had such a hard time teaching her what she needed to know for her adult life. She was able to use sources that she found to teach herself how to do these tasks in a memorable way.

Now that her kids are starting to enter their teens, she wants them all to have the knowledge of how to successfully take care of their home, especially her kiddos with ADHD. How does she make sure of that?

"Life Hacks" That Can Help Those Who Have ADHD

House management from one of Emma's children to the next might look different. Her typical brain children might do things differently from their siblings (who may also differ in house maintenance) and from each other. They may even find some of these tips helpful too! For those who have ADHD, these tips can make things really easy!

Cooking Tip: Use An Instant Pot For Making Meals

If your child has ADHD, this could be a great moving away present for when they move out. Instapots have the capacity to do a lot!

If your child struggles with cooking, it can help. A lot of Instapot recipes work by simply throwing a bunch of ingredients in the pot and setting it. While your child goes about their day, or they are at home relaxing, they can have their next meal cooking.

Set Up Your Kitchen Space So That Like Things Are Grouped Together

If you have ever worked a food service job, you might understand the importance of this right off the bat. Think about it. If you worked at a pizza place, it wouldn't make any sense to have dough on one side of the store, sauce on another, and then all of the toppings at another end of the store. It's all lined up for ease of use.

If you and your child are able to set up their home in a similar way, then it will make it easier. This might mean having the knives and cutting boards grouped together. It might mean that the spices are right next to the stove and oven. The baking dishes are stored under the oven, where a person can easily grab them. Water bottles are right next to the fridge, where you can grab one to fill it up. If you enjoy coffee or tea in the mornings, everything you need to make it is within your reach!

This makes it very easy to accomplish things in the morning. You don't have to spend time looking for something, and therefore, you have fewer opportunities to get distracted in the morning.

Easy Make Appliances

An Instapot is just one example.

The world comes up with a lot of crazy gadgets that we don't ever think we would need. There are apple slicers, strawberry pitters, Keurigs, electric kettles, panini makers, and more.

If it helps your teen, encourage them to get it for themselves. Whatever will help make things easier for them is worth the investment!

Organizational systems

Keep in mind that when your teen is off living on their own, they aren't going to have you there. This means that if they get distracted in the morning, you aren't going to pull them back and remind them that they need to be focusing on getting ready.

Part of this will be eliminating opportunities to get distracted from the task at hand. One of the things that can play a role in distraction is too many things that don't have a home. Clutter and mess can take up a lot of space and confuse the mind. Try to help them find places for their belongings as much as possible. When it's not possible, invest in a few spaces that are designated for clutter so that it's out of sight.

Color Code Everything!

The ADHD brain processes visual information the best. It's time to take full advantage of this. Color coding can go for your laundry baskets (different colors depending on whether it's lights, colors, or darks), drawers, and desk space; you name it.

If you are trying to color-code drawers in some way, use electrical tape. It sticks really well, but if you happen to be renting your space (or you just don't want to damage your property), they don't leave any damage behind. You can also buy it in fun colors.

Marie Kondo Methods

Let's talk about two ideas that Marie Kondo had that someone with ADHD can bring into their life.

The first is the method that she chooses for decluttering. Is the item serving a purpose? Have you used it in the last two weeks? Does it spark joy? If you can't answer anything here with a yes, then it needs to go. These three simple questions can help you decide whether or not to keep an item in your house. This streamlines the process, and it can help you get rid of so many things.

The next popular method she has is of folding things. When you follow this, items are folded in such a way that they can stand up when they are bunched together. This means that when you open a drawer, it's all visible. You can see everything you need for the occasion.

Once again, this can help someone with ADHD adhere to keeping things visual. It also helps them take more advantage of their wardrobe.

Make Use Of Visual Reminder Methods

One huge example of visual reminders is post-it notes. You can stick these anywhere, and they can remind you of things that are going on. Another example is using window markers, which are good for your mirror as well. You can write with them and then take them off like a window cleaner.

Maintaining a day-to-day life with the challenge of ADHD is manageable. You just need to know a few extra tips. Our next topic is similar.

Life Paperwork

No one tells us just how much paperwork is involved when you become an adult. We need to keep track of identity documents, financial documents, and so much more. How does your teen handle this?

First, there must be an organizational system. A filing cabinet is the best, most visual option for this. Use picture labels instead of writing it out if you can! Some things can now be kept digitally, which we are going to talk about below.

Identity Documents

This is your birth certificate, passport, social security card, and to some extent, your driver's license. Your teen's driver's license should be with them at all times. Everything else should be stored in a place that is as safe as possible. Try to lock it away if you can.

Some things on these lists can be stored online, but not these. There are watermarks and a host of security things stored within these documents that people will look for. You won't be able to find these things online.

Medical Documents

Medical documents are tricky. There are some that you shouldn't worry about, and some you should keep for a long time.

Many of your insurance documents can be scanned and uploaded online or to a server. The same is true for any yearly exam, be it physical, dental, or vision. Keep a physical copy of the most recent and have your teen add it to their filing system.

Medical bills (from hospitals) should be scanned ASAP. Your teen is going to want to retain physical copies at least until the debt is paid. Even after that, retain scanned copies, and your teen will want to be able to access them. Hospital investigations happen often, and your teen will want their documents in hand.

Your teen will also want to have physical documentation of their ADHD. Many employers are willing to accommodate, provided that there is proof that the person has the disorder. Doctor's notes, a record of diagnosis, or another legal/medical document that talks about their ADHD should suffice.

Housing Documents

This refers to anything related to your current housing situation. Today, most young adults rent their homes first. When you rent a home, you are going to want a copy of a renters agreement, bank statements, checklist, and information about devices in the house (like smoke detectors, carbon monoxide detectors, the dishwasher, etc.). Further, it is best to retain any safety procedures that the landlord would like followed, any legal issues that need to be tended to, and the checklist of damages that existed when they moved in.

Today, these documents may already exist online, in which case you have a pdf that you can easily keep track of. If the original copy is paper, though, you should save that for the duration that you live there.

Now, if they own a home, they are going to want all of your information for that as well. In this case, it doesn't need to be on hand. Owning a home is a more stable situation. If you damage something, you fix it without jumping through hoops. You will have a deed, but you won't need to sign legal forms with a landlord. And, you won't need to keep track of a housing contract, which many people have to do.

For these papers, having electronic copies is fine.

Car Documents

There are probably some good odds that your teen either has a car or has plans to get one in the future (even if it's the distant future). There will be a lot of documents for their vehicle, but what do you keep?

You will want to keep what the dealer gives you. Keep it in hard copy for about a year before you scan it and try to go digital with it.

You should also keep a copy of registration information, lease information if a loan was used, the title, and your insurance information.

Keep insurance information and registration information in the car. The rest can be filed until it can be digitized.

Purchase Receipts

There used to be a time when you would want to carry all of your receipts and keep a hold of them for your taxes. Electronic banking has mostly stopped this habit. In addition to always having access to the charges on your accounts, if you need a receipt, you can get one emailed to you.

For those who have ADHD, a pile of receipts can look like an overwhelming mess of clutter. It's hard to sort through, and they may not even need it. Receipts can be scanned and digitized if they would like, but they don't have to be.

The only time your teen should need to keep a receipt is if they made the purchase for his workplace. Any receipt copies don't have to be kept for more than three years.

Rental and Homeowner Repair and Renovation

If they live in a rental and something breaks or a renovation takes place, then the landlord usually pays for that, except in particular circumstances. For these, if they sign any agreements with the contracted company or the landlord, then they should keep either physical or scanned copies, just in case they are needed. They should only need to keep these for a year, though.

If they own a home, then this is going to look a little different. They are going to want to keep these records longer as they might matter when it comes to a tax return. The recommendation is to keep copies (physical or online) for about five years.

Pay Stubs

Most pay stubs are electronically delivered now. If your teen still gets paper stubs, they only need to keep them for about a year or until tax season comes.

Power, Water, and Other Utilities

The bills for these may be either online or in paper form. If they are online and you receive PDFs, then store those safely. They may also be found online through an account they have with the utility company, in which case they don't need to worry about it.

Most utility companies still send bills through the mail, though, so they may have paper copies to deal with. It's best to keep them for about a year. They might not need them for tax purposes, but your now-adult may need to check them for errors by comparing them, or you might notice that something extra is running in the house when it doesn't need to be, and it's driving your bills up.

Credit Card Information

You don't really have to keep these for too long. When your teen gets a credit card, teach them to check the statement to make sure that all of the charges are correct, and then they can be thrown away.

Property and Investment Information

Investments are an exciting topic and probably one you're going to want to discuss with your teen. The recommendation is to always start as soon as possible with at least a retirement investment.

Then, you might go bigger and continue to invest from there. Explain the purpose of investments so your teen understands. For these, they need to have a good hold of the investment information for about three years, just in case the IRS takes a look and asks for the info.

Properties aren't likely to be something your teen has right away unless they inherit something from the family, but they do fall into the same category as investments.

Tax records

If your teen is underage but has a job, they are going to have tax returns to deal with. You might be able to keep them online, so you don't have to deal with a paper copy, but you should keep hold of them for at least three years.

Loan Records

If your teen isn't 18 yet, they probably won't have these, but when they do, they should keep their payment records for up to three years and the record of a paid-off loan for seven years.

What To Do With All Of This Information?

Your teen probably doesn't have to deal with most of these things just yet, but they will soon! Given that information on these papers isn't common knowledge, it's all presented here.

When people get a hold of important papers, one of two things are bound to happen. They either keep it for twenty years or throw it away immediately. Having a system in place when your teen moves out can help avoid either of these.

Start devising one for your own papers and let your teen help. Seeing this model early can help them know what to do in the future.

When it comes time for your teen to move out, help them first set up a filing cabinet. With each file, have the information on what it contains, how long the items inside need to be kept, and the last date they went through it. If you, and later your teen, are able to set aside monthly time to go through these documents, a couple of folders at a time, then you can generally keep up on the paperwork that comes with life.

Clean Homes

It's often been said that people with ADHD are naturally messier. Maybe that's true; however, it doesn't mean that those with ADHD can't keep a clean home. If your teen is prone to mess, then let's look at some things that might help them.

Sort Through Mail and Papers Every Day

Mail and paperwork can pile up fast, and with ADHD, trying to sort through all of it at the end of the week just sounds awful and like a disaster waiting to happen. Now, if you do it each day, it won't pile up. You can model this behavior to your teen and let them know why you do it!

Have A Weekly Chore Plan

No one likes having to spend all day cleaning their house, and if you have ADHD, it might not get done at all. Instead of trying to do it all in one day, set up a weekly plan for what gets done and when.

You can do this in a planner or an app, but take time to sit with your teen, write down all of the chores that need to be done in the house, and write down when the day they are going to be done. When they still live at home, also write down who is going to do them. When your teen is on their own, they will already have this practice down!

Keep Laundry In the Laundry Room

In addition to being helped by color-coded baskets, your teen is likely to find some use in having it all in the laundry room. With the baskets right next to the washer, your teen can simply toss in the basket when it gets full and start it when they need to.

Kitchen Maintenance

First, try to have your teen make a habit of rinsing their dish every meal. By doing this, they are stopping the sink from becoming a problem. Next, have them make sure the dishwasher runs every night, and make it a point to have it be put away in the morning so that dirty dishes can go right in. Try not to purchase too many things that need to be hand-washed, as it just happens to make things more complicated.

Next, when teaching about a clean fridge, have them first understand the importance of fridge maintenance and teach them the smell test. Cleaning the fridge out at least once a month with disinfectant is essential, and your teen might be more engaged by listening to music or watching the difference between a dirty and clean fridge.

Bathrooms

A tip your teen might find helpful is to turn the water on for the shower and run it as hot as possible for about ten minutes. The steam this creates will loosen a lot of stain buildup.

Now with that done, most of the mess can be wiped away easily!

Understandably, having your teen living on their own might be a stressful time for you. It may help when they are set up and know how to take care of their home in the future. Right now, a lot of things probably seem like they are far off from happening, but the sooner we start modeling behaviors, the better they will be for the future.

Chapter Seven

I Can't Remember

ADHD often comes with memory deficits. When you learn that memory is also centered in the frontal lobe, that information probably won't surprise you.

Being able to remember important details is often essential to making sure that we are getting our work done in a timely fashion and that we are on top of things. Right now, you are likely primarily noticing your child's memory deficit in school. As they get into the workforce, it's likely to impact them there too. There are several methods in the school and working world that can help your teen get a head start and make up the slack that the frontal is creating. Starting to teach them now while they are in school can ensure that they become great habits in the future.

Some General Memory Tricks

Let's start with the basics.

Make An Emotional Connection

When your child is learning about something, one thing that can help them retain it is to make an emotional connection with the information. While this might be tough in math class, in classes like English and history, it's easy. English papers are written with emotion, and a personal story often gets the teacher's attention and stands out in a good way among the sea of papers they have to grade. Your child can also connect better to the material that they were working on.

In history class, your child might connect by learning about relatives or the emotional stories of people and what they experienced during significant historical events.

Make It Unique

When your child is struggling to pick up school material, help them by getting creative with how you might help them study it.

You can use Pinterest or google for some inspiration and go from there! Flashcards, rereading the text, and other traditional methods haven't been helping, so what will? The more creative the idea, the better it can be absorbed!

Get Your Senses Involved

When your teen is in school and receiving the information, they are already engaging two basic senses: sight and hearing. See if you can engage the other three. In science, perhaps they are learning about different smell reactions. If it's safe, see if you can create the small. In history, they might be learning about a new historical event. See if you can't find an area where they might be able to imagine themselves in that event.

Sensory experiences can go a long way in making our memory do its job and remember things. You are making up to five different connections with the material.

Make Use Of Movement

Motion can engage the memory as well.

Let's say, for example, that your child is looking to learn a complicated math formula. Put it on a dry erase board. Have them draw arrows, trace steps, and move their way through the process.

Use Mnemonics and Word Tricks

Schools often use this a lot already. You might have heard of PEMDAS or, Please Excuse My Dear Aunt Sally for the way to remember the proper order for basic math equations. These tend to stick in our minds because it's a pattern. For an odd reason, we tend to attach to those.

Create as many as you want and make them as wacky as you want. They tend to stick even better when you do.

Engage Your Focusing Skills

The frontal lobe also controls our ability to focus, and that can sometimes be the cause of our issues. Focus isn't just going to magically appear because we want it to, especially when ADHD is involved. Occasionally, we need to get creative about how we do this. One thing you can do is try to meditate. Spend some time focusing on nothing. When the time is up, your brain is refreshed, and you can try again!

Another thing you can try to do is engage a different part of your brain. An easy way to do this is to toss a ball between your hands and catch it. This repeated action makes it so that you can restructure your thoughts a bit.

Music can help. Try music with little to no words or a simple tune. Focus music that lasts for several hours can help with longer studying sessions.

If the problem is a lack of focus, then that part needs to be taken care of before anything else!

Take a Break and Get Some Fresh Air

If you have spent an hour trying to get the information together, then a t10 to 20-minute walk is likely in your best interest. The fresh air has a healing effect on our body, and it can remove the stress blocks from our mind that may be causing our memory to fall short. Furthermore, by taking the time to walk away, we are letting the jumbled information fall away from our brains.

It gives us a clean slate, and we can start over on our work. When we do this, the stress blocks are gone, and our brain gets to recreate the map of its thoughts. It may now create it in such a way that we can easily recall what we were initially struggling with.

Exercises For The Memory

There are many things that we can do in our environment and for ourselves that will help out memory.

Create A Dedicated Space For Your Teen To Work

We've talked about how this relates to other chapters, but let's explore its specific connection to memory.

Our brains respond differently depending on their environment. In a previous example, we talked about what happens when we go to a coffee shop. We might want to stop working, but there is a certain amount of peer pressure around us that won't let that happen. There is another factor in play as well.

Do you regularly go to a coffee shop to work? If you do, your brain has likely made this a "designated workspace." This means that your focus and work will improve, including the speed at which you do it and how well you might remember it.

If you are able to create a space like this in your teen's home, it can improve their memory.

In order to make this work, this space needs to only be dedicated to working. It's not going to be a space to also eat, for entertainment, or a space to sit and get ready for the day. Doing those things in this space can confuse the brain and lessen the effect that the area will have on the work.

Once this space is designated, try to make it as distraction-free as possible. Have all of the materials nearby. With an environment that is there to support their needs, your teen is likely to run into fewer problems overall.

Create Signals For The Brain

Allow me to introduce you to Ivan Pavlov. Pavlov is credited with the discovery of classical conditioning. In his experiment, he discovered that when a dog is presented with food (which causes them to start drooling) and another stimulus (a bell in this case), the dog will eventually associate the bell with food and will drool at the sound of the bell, even with no food present.

We are able to classically condition ourselves if we would like to. When it's time for your teen to study or do homework, with their permission, create something that leads to classical conditioning. In this case, you might try a particular white noise sound, like a fan or the ocean. You can also try focus music.

Whatever the sound is, start playing it a couple of minutes before they begin their homework or studying session. Then, continue to let it play as they work.

As a bonus, if your teen finds that they are struggling with focusing in school, they can play this sound to help them focus. You can have the doctor include this in their IEP or 504 plan.

Measure Out Progress and New Work

Having a way to quantify progress can help keep your teen from becoming discouraged.

A good, simple, visual way to do this is to keep a dry erase board in their study area. Using this dry-erase board on normal homework days might mean that you write down each subject and the work you are going to do for it. As you do the work, you cross it off until there is nothing left.

On days where one subject is particularly demanding or difficult, let that subject take over the board. Write down every little thing that has to be dealt with and cross it off one by one.

When they enter the workforce, this technique can be really helpful to them as well. Each time they complete a task they need to do or a part of a project, they can cross it off!

The visual is a reminder to the brain that, first of all, a lot has been done and that there is a lot to go!

Help Them Create A Mental Map Of The Work

Okay, so here is one of the good things about school. When you are introduced to a new topic, it often isn't completely new. It's likely linked to another topic that you studied in class. One way to help your teen remember all of this information is to link it together.

In math, this is easier because mathematical knowledge tends to build. Have your child start the new topic by reviewing previous, relevant material and drawing any needed connections. This starts up some background knowledge that will help them remember their new lessons, and it gives them material to draw from and connect to when they are struggling.

In English, your child is learning new things all about the same language. One thing you can do is have your child give examples of new concepts but always use the same reading. It can be an excerpt from their favorite book, which can be engaging, but use it to have them point out as many examples as possible about what they are learning. When there aren't any examples available, have them rewrite sentences about what they are learning.

In history, create a timeline. When did this news even happen? During what time period? Compared to other events, when did this fall?

Aim For Understanding Before They Memorize It

Your child may be able to memorize the entire math formula, and yet they might not understand anything about it. Before we have them memorize this information, they need to be able to comprehend it. What are some things we can do about this?

Have them work through parts of the sequence at a time. Have them draw things out or use objects to demonstrate. Have them try to relate it to themselves or other things in their life. There are quite a few options available, and the best one will depend on how your teen processes things.

Once you are sure that they fully understand the material, then you can dive into memorization strategies.

Practice

The saying "practice makes perfect" is absolutely true when it comes to remembering information.

Have your child practice as much as possible, and try to make it fun. Invest in a big dry erase board for math practice. Have them retry (safe) science experiments at home, or at least watch videos about the cool aspects of what they are learning.

In subjects like English and history, create a Kahoot and get their friends to play before a test. Kahoot is an online quiz game used by teachers. It ranks people by their correct answers and how fast they get them.

Anything that creates opportunities to practice what they are learning is going to improve their memory.

Create Info Sheets

These can be math formulas, scientific facts, the periodic table, a list of vocabulary, a history timeline, what different English sentence parts are, and whatever else your teen may need to stay on top of their studies. It might seem counterintuitive for their memory, but having it close by to stare at can help. It also stresses comprehension over basic meaning.

Understandably, you might wonder if this is going to be helpful in the long run, but most college tests are online and open-note, thanks to technology. Students are often allowed their notes too. Once they get a job, having notes on hand will likely be a part of it.

Now, in high school, things are a little more strict, but it's always worth it to talk to your teacher. In some cases, you might be able to get it into their IEP or 504.

Don't Forget The Highlighters.

Information is often better presented visually or verbally. It's rare for someone with ADHD to do their best work while staring at a block of text. Find colorful highlighters. Use a brand that has several different colors to offer.

Now, you can't usually write all over a school book. What you can do is attach translucent paper and highlight all over that. You might also be able to rent the book online and use that to make your highlights.

Your child can use whatever system of highlighting works best for them. They might choose to only highlight the important information. They might highlight every other paragraph or alternate colors on paragraphs so they have an easier time reading them. They may also highlight the topics within the chapter.

Highlighting doesn't have to be reserved for textbooks. Let your child feel free to highlight their notes, handouts, and homework as needed.

The simple act can help to make the information visual to your child.

Schedule Reviews

This can help make tasks like preparing for tests feel less daunting. Schedule different review times for each subject, and use these to revisit parts of the information your child has been learning.

You might use these times to go over the information that was harder for them to understand. You might use this time to go over things that maybe didn't make sense initially but do with the extra time. You might use this time to go over things they learned at the beginning of the unit that you know will still be on the test.

These review times can be serious, or a game can be made out of them. They can be conducted in the usual space your child has, or you can decide to go outside or to a park or a coffee shop. You can lead these, or your child can. Whatever route you take will depend on how your child's brain naturally processes information.

Study Your Teen's Style

You don't want to embark on this journey and discount the things that work well for your teen already. If they have certain things that they do that help them learn, work these into some of these tips. This is what your child's brain is already naturally doing. The goal is to enhance it.

These exercises start in school, and then they can continue into the adult world with your teen.

While your teen may not need the knowledge of every subject from school as they enter the adult world, there are skills like time and project management, information absorption, and memory techniques that they will take with them to the adult world. Their adult life and workplace may require it. What other skills about being a student can we teach that will help them in their adult life?

ADHD Study Tips

When your child brings home a bad grade, you might think that they just need more time than the average student to study. While this is a sensible explanation, it isn't an accurate one. An ADHD brain doesn't work like a traditional one, so traditional methods might not be of much help.

This is true now, and it will be true for their jobs later. What are some things that they can do?

Engage In Active Studying

This is something that experts in education recommend for college students, and it's especially helpful to people with ADHD. We discussed the weakness of the textbook for those with ADHD in a previous section. However, that is often the most popular method of studying.

Think instead of making tests, using flashcards, or doing group study. These methods feel overwhelming at first, but they lead to better retention in the long run. These are called active study methods, and it essentially forces your brain to engage with the information you have just given it.

Record Lectures

If you are worried that teachers won't allow recording, then try to get it into your teen's IEP or 504. Recording lectures means that, first of all, if your child feels that they missed important information, they have something to go back to. Second of all, if your child wants, they can listen to the lecture again, identify the important information, and get it either rewritten or highlighted in their notes. This is active learning as they are actively attending to and identifying the information.

Make Technology a Part Of the Routine

Technology has so much to offer the ADHD world. Many apps have been created to make our lives easier, and we should take advantage of them. There are note-taking apps like Notability, flashcard apps (like Chegg), and apps for quizzes (like Quizlet). Using technology for this can help to streamline the process and get your child working faster. Part of studying will be efficiency.

Don't Let Your Child Cram

Cramming is never a good strategy, especially when you have ADHD. First of all, if your teen plans to cram and save it all to the last minute, they have no backup for a bad day with their focus. Second, trying to study for long periods of time hurts everyone's focus. Third, spreading it out gives your teens a chance to better process things. Alternatively, have them stay on top of studying throughout the year. This way, there is little panic and routine disruption when a test is coming up.

Environment Tip: Essential Oil Diffuser

Using an essential oil diffuser can help your child focus if it's the right scent. Studies show that mint, citrus, and eucalyptus all have powerful focus effects. You can get a diffuser and let the smell come into the room for your teen to use. These smells may eventually also lead to a classical conditioning effect, and your child can easily take them to school and rub them on their wrist as needed.

These scents can also help with stress levels, especially when they are around comforting places for your teen.

Light Sugars

Our brain uses up a surprising amount of energy each day. Because your teen has ADHD, they might even be using double the amount of energy that their peers are for the same tasks. Because of this, their blood sugar might get low. It won't be low enough to cause a medical emergency, but it will be low enough to cause fatigue, restlessness, trouble focusing, and even a sick feeling.

Moderately sugary beverages can be a solution for this. Skip soda and energy drinks. Those will be too much, too fast. But a drink from Starbucks, a sip of apple juice, or a smoothie can provide the rise of blood sugar that your teen might need. When they have these, try to keep them from drinking them too fast. That won't help, and it will cause a sugar crash.

A huge struggle that many people with ADHD face is test-taking and learning. Now, in the adult world, there might not be tests, but there will be meetings, presentations, and more that they will need similar skills for. It's important to develop these skills as early as possible so that your teen enters the adult world with a sort of muscle memory of how to get through these tasks.

Our last chapter also talks about something that is important now and when your teen gets to the adult world. Right now, socializing is how they build up their friend circles and how they talk to their elders, teachers, and those younger than them. In the future, it will be about how they talk to customers, interact with coworkers, and forge relationships in the adult world.

Chapter Eight

Building Confidence and Social Skills

When her daughter was diagnosed with ADHD at the age of seven, Mary started to prepare. She studied all of the habits associated with ADHD. She was prepared for emotional explosions. She was prepared for the difficulty that her child would have in school. She was ready for the mess. From day one, she helped her daughter with all of these challenges, and she's happy to say that it worked, and her daughter now does fine in these areas. There is just one thing she didn't see coming, and as such, she felt completely unprepared for it.

Mary's daughter, Rose, is now 14. Mary started to notice some small changes in Rose when she was 12. She was quieter. When she turned 13, Mary noticed that when she offered praise, Rose didn't quite seem to believe her. Finally, one day, when Rose was struggling particularly badly because she couldn't focus, Mary pulled her away from work and tried to remind her about some of the good things about

ADHD. Rose screamed at her mother to stop before she ran to her room and slammed the door. Mary was shocked. She thought she had done a decent job in highlighting the positive aspects.

When she was able to talk to Rose the next day, she got the truth. Rose wasn't struggling with her ADHD because of issues focusing. She was struggling because it made her different from her peers. They didn't seem to think as she did, and it made the whole thing incredibly difficult. Not only that, but she noticed that she had a hard time either keeping up with a conversation or not getting ahead of it. Her friends seemed annoyed sometimes, and it was really affecting her.

This isn't something we think about when we think of ADHD, but the impact it can have is huge, especially in the teen years. With ADHD, this can also become a hyperfocus issue, and if that happens, it can affect them well into adulthood. The teen years are a time when self-esteem is especially vulnerable as well.

Because of ADHD, social skills can be harder to pick up. It can be harder to read the room and focus on a conversation. This can affect how people perceive a person, and that can cause severe self-esteem issues. On top of that, we have to think of the effect of ADHD as a label. Positive talk at home may only be able to do so much when the world is a cruel place. For that reason, this chapter is dedicated to the social and emotional effects of ADHD and how to combat them.

Tips For Developing Social Skills In Teens

Guidance In The Moment

Guidance is especially helpful when your teen is younger (though it works at any age). You likely often see your teen interacting with others and working. You might notice when things are off with their behavior and when it doesn't fit into social situations.

When you notice this, pull them aside. Gently go over what they did and how it didn't fit, and then advise them on a better strategy for next time. Try something like, "Hey, I was watching you talk to that person, and when they were telling a sad story, you tried to make a joke. I know you were probably just trying to lighten the mood and make them feel better, but instead of doing that, it actually hurt them and made them think you weren't listening. Maybe try some words of encouragement?"

This isn't going to be a comfortable talk for your teen, so managing your tone and trying to make them as at ease as possible will help with the reception of the information.

If you notice a lot of issues within a short time period, it might be a good idea to make a note and talk to them right after the event instead of during it.

Roleplay

Your child might struggle with specific situations. If they come to you with troubles or if you notice them, suggest a roleplay. This can give them a chance to walk through different ways of responding and help them get a chance to practice and test out different behaviors. The next time they need to deal with this specific social situation, they are ready and know how to handle it appropriately.

Facial Expressions

Facial expressions that come naturally to you might not come so naturally to your teen. There are a couple of ways to help with this. One method is the use of facial expression charts. Elementary children often use this when they are first learning, and it can be incredibly helpful for children with ADHD as well.

Another thing you can do is watch TV with your teen and point out different facial expressions. Going back to behavior, you can also use TV to demonstrate actions that are appropriate and actions that aren't.

Goal Setting

Goal setting is helpful in dealing with a lot of issues that are the result of ADHD, including social situations. A goal can look like paying close attention to a line of conversation, being more empathetic, or making sure that others also have a chance to speak. Help your teen find measurable ways to achieve these goals and then set them.

Give Them A Lot Of Opportunity To Practice

I understand that there is a certain temptation to have them stay home as much as possible when they tend to have issues with social environments, especially if those issues lead to emotional explosions, but we are all trying to raise our kids to be successful adults, and that will hurt them in the long run. Doing the opposite is actually going to be more helpful.

Get your teen used to social situations and proper cues. The more they are able to get out and practice and work on it, the better off they will be in the future.

When you are looking for different things to try with your teen, look for things that will interest them. Find conferences and conventions for their hobbies. Have them join sports and clubs that they like. Find groups that cater to their interests. All of these will be engaging so that social practice doesn't feel like a chore, and it will provide practice for social engagement.

Play To Their Strengths

Each brain and each case of ADHD is going to be different. There are going to be some things that they do really well and some things that they will need to work on. As they navigate these challenges, they are going to hear a lot of feedback about the things they need to work on, and that feedback isn't always going to be kind. If you find that after an event, you're going to have to talk about a lot of things that went wrong, try to add some balance. Throw in things that they did right as well. Not only does this help delivery and prove that you're not just watching their mistakes, but it also provides positive reinforcement.

Another thing that might help is finding an outlet for their more challenging behaviors. If you notice, for example, that your teen tends to be opinionated and tends to try and argue with relatives over a difference of opinion, suggest they join a debate club. This is an outlet that will give this ability a chance to have an outlet, and they can learn a lot at this club, including more social skills.

Talk To Them

This one seems so simple, as we talk to each other every day. But, how often do we sit and have a conversation with little to no distraction?

Invest in the time to do this with your teen as much as possible, or at least once a week. It will help them with these skills, and as they get older and when they do grow up, you will be glad you set aside this time.

Talk To Them About Sensitive Topics

When someone is struggling with ADHD, it can be hard to sort out their thoughts on big topics.

At the time of writing this, news headlines are lit up with major controversial topics, and that's unlikely to change at any point in the future.

With so much news on highly charged topics floating around, your teen might have trouble sorting through all of their thoughts on these issues.

Sit down and ask them what in the news stands out. If there are a lot of things, have them write them down. Then, ask them about their feelings, followed by their thoughts. Give them space to work through these, and try not to influence them to think one way about something, as it can make it harder on the brain.

Practice Their Listening Skills

This is a big one. It can be hard for those with ADHD to actively pay attention to conversations, even if it's one they are involved in. It can also be hard for them to stop talking, especially if their brain gets on a train of thought. Try to both model this behavior, and give them gentle reminders when needed.

When someone has ADHD, they are capable of many things, including big ideas. This serves them well in the adult world so long as they are able to communicate their ideas.

Social skills can be a lifelong learning process for everyone. It's easy to blame that needed learning on ADHD interference and let it hurt your self-esteem. The teen years are a point where your child might be especially vulnerable to this, and that can carry to adulthood. How do we prevent it?

Tips To Help Your Teen Boost Self Esteem

Self-esteem gets more important the older your teen gets. Low self-esteem is tied to issues with self-worth, as well as mental health issues such as anxiety and depression.

Because of their brain's issue with dopamine production, people with ADHD are already prone to mental health struggles. There are steps that can be taken in the home to help!

Be Mindful Of Self-Talk

Self-talk is your inner voice. How you think about yourself and the words you would use to describe yourself is a part of self-talk.

When we have negative self-talk, we tend to put ourselves down. We might ignore the good qualities we have and put way too much emphasis on qualities we see as being bad.

You might notice that your teen has negative self-talk if they seem to either talk a lot about themselves using negative language or if they make comments like "I'm not smart," "I'm useless," or "I can't seem to do anything right."

If you notice this about your teen, try to work on positive self-talk. Affirmations can be a great way to encourage positive self-esteem. Another thing you can try is reframing. If your teen makes a negative comment about themselves, have them stop and rethink it. Rephrase the statement in a way that encourages positive self-talk.

Is Your Teen Kind To Themself?

One thing that your teen is going to need to remember is that they have ADHD, and because of that, they might have to do twice the work to get the same result as their friend. When they accomplish something, they should be proud of themselves that they were able to get that result.

What might happen a lot of the time is that they are upset because the extra effort feels like a reflection of their ability. It's not. Teach your teen to celebrate their victories, acknowledge that some things are going to be harder, and celebrate when those things are taken care of.

Have Patience

When your teen gets frustrated with themselves, try to use strategies to steer them toward a more peaceful line of thought. Your teen might expect the same results that everyone else gets from the same level of effort. Remind them that it's okay to have patience for yourself. It's okay if things take a little more effort.

Don't Make a Habit Of Comparing People.

Do you notice that when they are struggling, your teen might say something like, "all of my friends do fine with this material." or "they are able to control themselves in class with ease. I can't do that."

When you see that, make it a point that everyone is different, or point out things that they do really well that others can't.

If they compare themselves to others, they might end up in a battle with their self-esteem.

Our teens are growing human beings that are becoming adults very soon! With adulthood comes certain social graces and having the confidence to get through the world.

Review Page

Hi there,

  I hope you enjoyed the book! if you did and think it would benefit someone else.

  Please spread the word and leave a review, if you share the book and it brings value to others, then they will be so grateful for your help and you will feel great for helping another person with their challenges.

Conclusion

It can be hard to think about your teen heading into the adult world. Not only are they your baby, but they also have ADHD, and you still see some struggles.

Hygiene, which we talked about in chapter one, is one such struggle. Your teen might be putting it off to the last second because of issues with focus, sensory troubles, or thinking that no one is going to care. In the first chapter, we talked about several strategies that can help this process.

Along with proper hygiene, there is the need to keep the body healthy. If the body doesn't want to work, then neither will anything else. It also can be a preventative measure for severe ADHD symptoms. In chapter two, we talked about diet, exercise, and cooking healthy meals.

If your teen is still struggling with emotional control, you might be very worried about them moving out. Part of emotional control is making use of resources around you, like a 504 plan. There are also strategies that you can use in the meantime to cool off.

Another aspect of both the teen and adult world is organization and time management. Both of these might look different to someone with ADHD. They will need different methods and strategies, but when they find something that works for them, then that is something they should stick with!

Impulsivity might become an even bigger issue when money gets involved. In chapter five, we talk about impulsivity with money and ensuring that financial decisions are made with intention. We also talk about how to set up a visual budget with ADHD.

In chapter six, we discussed home and adult life maintenance. There are many things that we don't even think about as teens that involve home and paperwork. Knowing how to take care of these things can save a lot of hassle down the road!

Finally, the issues of memory, confidence, and social skills are handled in chapters seven and eight. These are considered soft skills, which are always best to be taught as soon as possible. They can help make your teen's adult life easier, and it helps them on their journey in both their teen years and their adulthood.

ADHD or not, your teen is going to go on to do amazing things. With your help, they will have the skills they need to get by.

I hope you can take something from this book and set your kiddo up for success in life. If so please don't forget to leave a review so this book reaches as many parents as possible many thanks Kenneth

Other Books By Kenneth Harvey

References

8 Basic Cooking Skills Every Budding Chef Must Know. (2019, January 3). The ICCA Stockpot. https://iccadubai.ae/stockpo t/8-basic-cooking-skills-every-budding-chef-must-know

American Academy of Child and Adolescent Psychiatry. (2019). ADHD & the Brain. Aacap.org . https://www.aacap.org/AACAP/Families_and_Youth/Facts_ for_Families/FFF-Guide/ADHD_and_the_Brain-121.aspx

Bean, S. (n.d.). *Poor Hygiene in Children: "My Kid Stinks!"* Empowering Parents. https://www.empoweringparents.co m/article/poor-hygiene-in-children-my-kid-stinks-help/

Bernstein, S. (2021). *ADHD and Your Emotions: Tips to Help You Manage Them*. WebMD. https://www.webmd.com/add -adhd/emotion-stress

Bhandari, S. (2020). *Get Organized: Tips For Living With Adult ADHD*. WebMD. https://www.webmd.com/add-adhd/ss/slid eshow-adhd-living-tips

Brittany. (2018). *ADHD & Keeping up with Hygiene,* Keep Calm and Grow On. https://keepcalmgrowon.com/adhdandhygiene/

CHADD. (2018). *Relationships & Social Skills,* CHADD. https://chadd.org/for-adults/relationships-social-skills/

Cruger, M., & Ph.D. (2006, October 6). *15 Memory Exercises for Forgetful Kids.* ADDitude. https://www.additudemag.com/working-memory-exercises-for-children-with-adhd/

Dolin, A., & M.Ed. (2016, November 28). *10 Secrets to Studying Smarter with ADHD.* ADDitude. https://www.additudemag.com/slideshows/how-to-study-with-adhd-and-ace-even-tricky-exams/

Editors, Add. (2016, November 28). *13 Clutter Hacks for the Easily Overwhelmed.* ADDitude. https://www.additudemag.com/slideshows/quick-cleaning-tips-for-the-easily-overwhelmed/

Flaxington, B. (2015). *5 Ways to Stop Beating Yourself Up.* Psychology Today. https://www.psychologytoday.com/us/blog/understand-other-people/201505/5-ways-stop-beating-yourself

Gunnars, K. (2018, July 24). *Mediterranean Diet 101: A Meal Plan and Beginner's Guide.* Healthline. https://www.healthline.com/nutrition/mediterranean-diet-meal-plan

Hallowell, E., & M.D. (2013, October 24). *Anger Is Important — But Only When It's Managed.* ADDitude. https://www.additudemag.com/anger-management-techniques-for-children-with-adhd/

Harveston, K. (2019, December 9). 7 ADHD Mindfulness Exercises for Kids, Teens and Adults. The Mindful

Word. https://www.themindfulword.org/2019/mindfulness
-exercises-adhd/

How to ADHD. (2021). *ADHD Friendly House Hacks - Feat. MY HOUSE! (Executive Function Friendly Tips).* On YouTube. https://www.youtube.com/watch?v=posZhu_YIl0

https://www.facebook.com/verywell. (2019). *Helping Your Teen With Time Management for a Successful Life.* Verywell Family. https://www.verywellfamily.com/teaching-time-ma nagement-skills-to-teens-2608794

Jackson, M. (2021, March 23). *When to Keep and When to Throw Away Financial Documents.* Her-Money. https://hermoney.com/earn/taxes/when-to-throw -away-financial-documents/

Joanne. (n.d.-a). *How Can a Child With ADHD Improve His or Her Memory? Thinking through ADHD.* Retrieved June 18, 2022, from http://thinkingthroughadhd.com/index.php/2018/07/ 27/how-can-a-child-with-adhd-improve-his-or-her-memory/

Joanne. (n.d.-b). *How Can Parents & Teachers Help ADHD Teens Fit in Socially?* Thinking through ADHD. https://thinkingthroughadhd.com/index.php/2018/12/29/h ow-can-parents-teachers-help-adhd-teens-fit-in-socially/

Josel, L. (2020, October 13). *Q: "What's the Best Way to Study for a Test with ADHD?"* ADDitude. https://www.additudemag .com/how-to-study-adhd-test-prep/

Kholberg, J. (2006, October 6). *Shortcuts to a Cleaner, Less Cluttered House.* ADDitude. https://www.additudemag.com/ housekeeping-made-easy/

Kolberg, J. (2006, October 6). *33 ADHD-Friendly Ways to Get Organized.* ADDitude. https://www.additudemag.com/how-to-get-organized-with-adhd/

Lang, S. (2022). *Cornell scientists help to develop Asian Diet Pyramid,* Cornell Chronicle. https://news.cornell.edu/stories/1996/01/cornell-scientists-help-develop-asian-diet-pyramid

Luria, Y. C. (2017, October 25). *What To Do When Your ADHD Child Has Poor Hygiene.* Blocked to Brilliant. https://blockedtobrilliant.com/your-adhd-child-has-poor-hygiene/

Moak, D. (2021, March 12). *7 Simple Cooking Tips and Tricks for Beginners,* Eating Europe. https://www.eatingeurope.com/blog/7-simple-cooking-tips-tricks/

Saline, S. (2021, February 10). *5 Ways to Reframe Anxiety for Your Worried Teen. ADDitude.* https://www.additudemag.com/anxiety-in-teens-adhd-reframing-skills/

Saline, S., & Psy.D. (2018, August 22). *Q: How Do I Teach My Teen to Manage Emotions?* ADDitude. https://www.additudemag.com/adhd-teen-managing-emotions/

Schreier, J. (2020). *Helping a child with ADHD develop social skills.* Mayo Clinic Health System. https://www.mayoclinichealthsystem.org/hometown-health/speaking-of-health/helping-a-child-with-adhd-develop-social-skills#:~:text=One%20of%20the%20most%20effective

Shannon, M. (2018, July 7). *Hygiene in ADHD Kids: Teaching Independence.* Miss Shannon's Cat Farm. http://cat-farm.com/hygiene/

Teaching Teens with ADHD Money Management. (n.d.). Www.brain balance centers.com. Retrieved June 18, 2022, from https://www.brainbalancecenters.com/blog/teaching-teens-with-adhd-money-management

Thomas, A. (2020, December 15). *10 Easy Ways To Get Kids Excited About Cooking, According To Experts.* Delish. https://www.delish.com/kitchen-tools/a34749087/10-easy-ways-to-get-kids-excited-about-cooking-according-to-experts/

U.S. Department of Agriculture. (2020). MyPlate | U.S. Department of Agriculture. Www.myplate.gov. https://www.myplate.gov/

Willard, C. (2018, March 9). *Teen Stress Is Very Real — and Manageable with These Exercises.* ADDitude. https://www.additudemag.com/slideshows/mindfulness-exercises-for-teens-adhd/

Wise, R. (2017, April 26). *23 Time Management Tips to Increase Productivity in Teenage Students with ADHD.* Education and Behavior. https://educationandbehavior.com/studying-tips-for-adhd-students/

World Health Organisation. (2021). *Healthy diet.* Www.who.int. https://www.who.int/initiatives/behealthy/healthy-diet#:~:text=A%20 healthy%20 diet%20is%20essential

WriterMay 10, E. B., & 2011. (2020). *Five Tips for Time Management for ADHD Children and Teens - Daily Life - ADHD.* W w w . h e a l t h c e n t r a l . c o m . https://www.healthcentral.com/article/managing-adhd-symptoms-five-tips-for-time-management-for-children-and-teens

Made in the USA
Las Vegas, NV
22 June 2023

73750775R00090